Joys and Subtleties

South East Asian Cooking

Joys and Subtleties

SOUTH EAST ASIAN COOKING

ROSEMARY BRISSENDEN

PANTHEON BOOKS

A Division of Random House, New York

Library of Congress Catalog Card Number: 74-120901

ISBN: 0-394-40166-2

Manufactured in the United States of America

FIRST AMERICAN EDITION

To

D. W. C. NORTHFIELD

who made this book possible

and to

BOB

who eats it all and loves

Unless otherwise stated, the recipes in this book serve 2–3 people when only one dish is being prepared, and 6–8 when there are four or five dishes all told.

Acknowledgements

RECIPES are very much part of a local folk process. If they are transplanted into an alien environment, they have to be nursed into it carefully. I could never have attempted this task without the help of many people who know the terrain, as well as some who have spent most of their lives crossing cultures one way or another.

The people of Indonesia first taught me to like South East Asian food. Ailsa Zainu'ddin and some Colombo Plan students at Melbourne University led me to see that it was possible to cook it in foreign countries.

I am profoundly grateful to Elaine McKay and to Theo Meier, both of whom were living in the area when this book was being written, and were unfailingly generous in their help and care for the enterprise.

My thanks extend also over many cities and a number of countries. They go to Tati Achdiat, Johanni Johns, Clare Golson, Alice Ehr-soon Tay, Janet Penny, Jaya Subramaniam – all still of Canberra, and Tasnee Sarikananda Western, Chusook Wasiksiri, Mrs K. Charuvastra, and Mrs Mercy Abeyawickrema, who were there for a time. Many ladies of the Australian-Indonesian Association in that city have helped. I owe much to Anna Abeyagunawardene of Sydney. I am especially grateful to Dahlan Thalib and Wennie Dahlan of Djakarta; But Muchtar and Arnati But of Bandung; Rajes Thambiah in Singapore; Mrs Rajasooria, and Chrys Teh of Sarikat Lever Bros., in Kuala Lumpur; Lee Kok Liang and Mrs Lee of Penang; Mrs Wilhelmina Sim and Che Hafsah Harun of Kuching; and Gladys Boon and her family in Bangkok. Joan Beltz was very kind to me there, too.

Gehan Wijeyewardene provided a number of Thai terms for the Glossary, David Penny made some helpful comments on reading the introductions, and Joy Warren was a most intelligent typist.

7

My task would not be complete without recording my thanks to my husband. He helped enormously not only by being an honest critic and occasional secretary, but also by remaining cheerful throughout the eighteen months that saw the birth of two children as well as of this book.

Table of Contents

A Note on this American Edition

This book has been especially adapted for the American audience. British weights and measures have been converted into their American equivalents. Sources for obtaining unusual products mentioned in the recipes are given for most large American cities; a reliable mail-order source is also given; and, wherever possible, substitute or alternate ingredients are listed.

Weights and Measures

The following table gives equivalent measures used throughout the book.

A dash or pinch	$\frac{1}{16}$ teaspoon
1 teaspoon	$\frac{1}{3}$ tablespoon
3 teaspoons	1 tablespoon
4 tablespoons	$\frac{1}{4}$ cup
5$\frac{1}{3}$ tablespoons	$\frac{1}{3}$ cup
8 tablespoons	$\frac{1}{2}$ cup
16 tablespoons	1 cup
1 cup	$\frac{1}{2}$ pint
2 cups	1 pint
2 pints	1 quart
4 ounces	$\frac{1}{4}$ pound
8 ounces	$\frac{1}{2}$ pound
12 ounces	$\frac{3}{4}$ pound
16 ounces	1 pound

Introduction to
South East Asian Food

AMONGST the notable cuisines of the world the one which has received least attention is that of South East Asia. Yet few regional cooking styles are more attractive. The finest South East Asian dishes exhibit that respect for the innate qualities of the basic ingredients which is the mark of Chinese cooking. At the same time they are characterized by the blended subtlety of fragrance and flavour that is a feature of Indian curries. But although related to each of these styles of cookery, South East Asian cuisine has a distinct character of its own.

It has been widely recognized in other fields that the region has a basic unity. Historians write of the common imprint of the great Indian and Chinese civilizations of earlier periods. Geographers show that this is the area of 'mush' growth rather than the 'husk' of North and West Asia – rice and fruit and vegetables rather than dry grains; regular in climate instead of dramatically seasonal. Finally, sociologists stress what is probably most important: in spite of all outside influences, South East Asian societies and cultures have uniformly maintained a basic structure of their own; they have assimilated what has been useful from abroad without becoming swamped by the notions of others. Many of the original elements of the ancient native cultures still assert themselves.

The food of the area fits very neatly into this picture. The countries which have been placed in the region by experts in geography, history and the social sciences turn out to be identifiable in much the same way by the student of cookery.

The countries generally regarded as belonging to South East Asia are Indonesia, Malaysia, Thailand, Indo-China, Burma, and sometimes Ceylon. In this book I have deliberately chosen to exclude the two countries on the extreme edges of the region,

13

Burma and Indo-China, because they have been influenced more directly than the others by their immediate and powerful neighbours, India and China respectively. I have concentrated on Indonesia, Malaysia and Thailand, since I believe that it is here that we can find what can most specifically be called South East Asian food. Through a study of the food of these countries we should be able to isolate the elements of a South East Asian regional style of cooking.

To begin with they share a common group of ingredients. Those which belong exclusively to this group are lemon grass, laos and blachan (a kind of preserved fish or shrimp paste). All three of these are used extensively in the recipes which follow. The other ingredients are rice as the staple, chillies, garlic and onions, coconut milk, a wide variety of fruits and vegetables, fresh fish, some meat, and dried fish preparations of many sorts. What is specifically local about these is the *way* they are used – generously where they can be afforded, and without the shackles of strict food orthodoxy.

This lack of orthodoxy is the second basic element of the South East Asian style of food. Let me quote an example to illustrate what I mean. Garlic and onions play a part in Indian cooking, but in South India, where the orthodox Hindu culture is sustained, too great a use of these is considered impure. Meat and eggs are also anathema to the Brahmins, pillars of Hindu civilization, as meat is to orthodox Buddhists. However, the syncretism of these religions in South East Asia allows their members to be much more relaxed about the business of eating. South East Asian Hindus and Buddhists don't always uphold the rules. Even the nominal Moslems of Java and to a lesser extent the Moslems of Sumatra and Malaysia are sometimes a little free and easy in their attitude to pork, which is proscribed by their holy books. Orthodoxy has only a precarious hold in South East Asia, and the result of this is to be seen in the variety of the food it has to offer.

The third main characteristic of South East Asian food is its colour. This is the result not only of its variety and abundance but of the meticulous and often ritualistic manner in which it is

14

presented. The fact that seasonal and cyclic festivals associated with the planting and harvesting of rice are occurring all the time, and that animistic ceremonies and festivals have to be fitted in alongside the more orthodox religious rituals tends to make life for many South East Asians a perpetual round of feast occasions. And, of course, food and the arrangement of food reflect this most closely. Long and patient hours go into the skilful arts of food decoration. Many of the dishes that I have described would show this if they were being prepared in their homelands rather than in the relatively soul-less kitchens of the Western World.

This book gives no recipes for sweets and puddings for the reason that main meals in South East Asia do not include them. A meal will usually end with fresh fruit, which is the best possible conclusion to a repast of such tonal quality. While splendid South East Asian sweets and cakes do exist, they are usually enjoyed as snacks and between-meal indulgences. They are most often made commercially and sold in shops and markets.

I am well aware that no Occidental cook can hope to reproduce exactly the dishes that are prepared in South East Asia. To attempt to do so, though, can be a rewarding experience. This book is meant to serve as a guide to those who wish to try. If it also conveys some sense of a rich and diverse culinary tradition I shall be very happy.

Utensils, Cooking Methods
and Ingredients, Glossary

Utensils

THE basic piece of apparatus in an Asian kitchen is the *open charcoal stove*. It is on the top of this that all the cooking is carried out. The poorest families use a simple fire outdoors; those who can afford it may have a multi-burner kerosene stove. Almost nowhere will you find an oven as we know it or an electric broiler.

In practical terms the nature of the traditional equipment has very much influenced the cooking habits of South East Asian countries. Oven-roasting or oven-baking is unknown in this part of the world. What you find instead is either roasting over the fire in banana leaves or deep-frying in oil. Broiling as we know it is replaced by barbecuing – a much more tasty method anyway, as we have recently come to realize. But the most common cooking methods are either boiling, simmering or frying the food on the top of the stove.

Apart from actual cooking with liquids, other methods have been used over the centuries in pre-industrial societies to preserve and break down food. These are all well known to anthropologists but not always familiar to Western cooks. They are smoking, salting and rotting. Foods which are prepared in these ways all find a place in this book, though they usually appear as imported condiments used for flavouring in cooking.

No major problems accompany the conversion of a Western kitchen to allow for cooking Asian style. It is a matter more of ignoring equipment than of adding to it, and all methods of Asian cookery can be adapted to what is at hand to cook with. Things that should be barbecued *can* be cooked under a broiler or, if large (like a whole chicken), in the oven: those that are

17

described as being baked in banana leaves are just as easily wrapped in foil and put in the oven. (Some households these days sport an outdoor or portable barbecue anyway.)

The pieces of equipment that are really vital are the rounded shallow pan with a curved bottom known usually in this country as a *wok*, but called a *kuo* in China, and some kind of grinding apparatus. All over South East Asia the wok, or *kwali* (the Indonesian name), is the basic kitchen utensil. Rice is cooked in it by the evaporation method, see p. 20. Curries and simmered dishes are made therein, often with the wok uncovered. Its shape allows for just the right kind of fairly rapid evaporation that is usually required. The initial frying of spices to which liquids are to be added is well accommodated by its contours. The wok makes deep frying much less problematic than it is in one of the conventional Western saucepans. You find you use much less oil this way, and the temperature remains more even and predictable.

As for grinding apparatus, this is a matter of great moment, for in South East Asian cooking spices, both dry and fresh, are usually ground together right down to a paste. Chopping, mincing or grating never achieves the same effect. In Indonesia the grinding is done with a wooden or stone pestle rubbed on a particularly hard, rough, hollowed out stone base. Malayans use a stone roller on a flat base. I have not seen either type of grindstone here. They are far too heavy for the plane-traveller to slip into a corner of her bag. And besides it must be admitted that they are difficult to use successfully unless you have had long practice and have developed the right muscles.

I have found that a successful and indeed far easier substitute for grinding spices is the *electric blender*. It grinds dry seeds to a powder in very quick time, and you can go on to achieve the paste by adding any fresh spices roughly chopped – nuts, garlic, onion, ginger, trasi, chillies, one at a time. One change in the Asian cooking method is often necessary, however. Usually Indonesians or Malays grind the spices to a paste in the way I have previously described, then either heat a little oil in a wok and fry them before adding other ingredients or add them straight to a water or coconut milk broth. If you use an electric blender you may often have to add some extra liquid as the blades turn in order to keep all the ingredients moving in the machine and blending. When this is the case, take note of how the recipe is meant to proceed (are the spices to be fried or simmered?) and add the liquid which is appropriate – oil if they are to be fried, water or coconut milk if they are to be simmered. There is no problem if the next step is to simmer the spices. Just proceed as usual. But if they are to be fried make sure that *you add no extra oil* when you put the paste into a heated pan on the stove. The oil you have used in the blender will produce the necessary frying action.

Useful but of less importance in the kitchen devoted to South East Asian cooking would be at least one *Chinese cleaver* – preferably two of the same size – and a *large, sharp chef's knife*. It doesn't have to be a heavy French one, as most often you will be cutting vegetables or slicing meat fine. There are some excellent light-weight Japanese knives which have a suitable wedge-shaped blade and are sharp.

You will find all sorts of uses for your cleaver. Chinese cooks use them for everything. They bone chickens, slice things, mince and chop with extraordinary facility, no matter how delicate the operation. The rapidity with which they work is quite terrifying to watch, although they never seem to lose their fingers.

Methods and Conventions in
South East Asian Cooking

HOW TO COOK RICE

In my experience, the cooking of rice is a subject that can arouse undreamt-of passions in otherwise mild people. For this reason it is usually avoided – like religion or politics – as a topic of polite conversation. However, I firmly recommend the evaporation method. Rice is the staple food in South East Asia, and the evaporation system of cooking it is the one that is always used there. Once you have mastered this procedure you will find that it never fails to yield a good, clean mound of rice in which the grains are separate, but at the same time soft without being at all clammy.

Take good quality white rice (long grain for preference) and wash it in a strainer until the water that runs through is no longer cloudy. Thorough washing is important because the particles of loose starch clinging to the outside of the raw rice must be removed. If they are not, they will produce the effect that we know so well in the laundry.

Place the washed rice in a heavy-bottomed saucepan with a tight-fitting lid and add cold water until it is an inch above the rice (a saucepan is just as good as a wok for the cooking of rice). No matter how much rice you use, nor how large the saucepan, the water-covering of approximately one inch is always the right amount. Add salt if you want to, though I personally find that it spoils the flavour of the rice.

Bring rapidly to the boil over a high heat, leaving the lid on loosely. Boil for approximately 10 minutes, or until the water has *all* been absorbed and the steam is escaping in single bubbles through holes in the surface of the rice. When I describe the water as being totally absorbed, that is just what I mean. *There should be no liquid left beneath the surface of the rice.*

Now place an asbestos mat under the saucepan, adjust the lid to fit tightly, and turn the heat to low for a further 10 minutes. Then – if you are cooking on an electric stove – transfer the saucepan and asbestos mat to another hot plate which you have just turned on. This ensures that you are using the lowest possible heat your stove will allow. Of course, if you are using gas, there will be greater heat control and you will not need to transfer the pan.

Leave the rice on low heat for about 20 minutes. It is now ready to use but can be left off the stove to keep warm in its own steam for a while.

HOW TO MAKE AND USE COCONUT MILK

Most people think that if they do not live in the tropics they might as well throw away all the recipes using coconut milk as soon as they see them. This is not so. The coconut milk that is used in cooking in South East Asia is made as a result of soaking grated fresh coconut flesh in water and squeezing out the juice. It can quite easily be produced in places without access to really fresh coconuts by using either of the following methods:

1. There are a number of commercial coconut cream preparations. In some stores in Australia you find packages of frozen coconut cream (called Lo-Lo) from Fiji. On the West Coast of the United States and in fancy-food stores and gourmet departments of supermarkets across the country, there is tinned coconut milk from Hawaii. These are both thick and can be watered down to produce the thin milk.

2. A cheap way to make thin coconut milk is to take 4 cups grated coconut meat and cover it with 2 cups boiling water. If you have an electric blender, transfer the coconut mixture to it and switch on, using medium speed, while you count to twenty. If you do not have a blender, allow the coconut to soak in the hot water for 20 minutes. In either case the final step is the same – pour the mixture into a bowl through a fine strainer or double thickness of cheese-cloth, squeezing the coconut hard in the strainer until no

21

juice remains. Discard the spent coconut pulp, add a pinch of salt to the liquid in the bowl, and it is ready for use.

Where a recipe specifies both thick and thin coconut milk, you could use this as an all-purpose one instead. Thus '1 cup of thick coconut milk and 2 cups of thin' becomes '3 cups of general-purpose coconut milk.'

When cooking with thick coconut milk there are two things to remember. Always stir it as it comes to the boil, and do not cover the saucepan while cooking. If either of these precautions is neglected, the dish will curdle.

HOW TO MAKE FRIED ONION FLAKES

Commercially prepared dried chopped onion provides the easiest raw material. Heat peanut or coconut oil (enough to cover the onion when it goes in) in a pan or wok until it is very hot. Drop in the dried onion and remove the pan from the flame immediately. Lift out the onion with a pancake turner before it burns, and drain on paper toweling.

In the absence of the dried kind, you can make fried onion flakes using fresh onions. Skin onions, cut them in half across (if you are using large ones) and then slice thinly and evenly lengthwise. Spread them out and allow them to stand and dry out for a few hours if possible. Heat a little peanut or coconut oil in a pan and when it is hot spread the onions out thinly in it. Turn the heat low and allow the onion flakes to cook brown and crisp on one side. Turn them carefully and allow to become brown and crisp on the other side. Watch the pan closely throughout, to make sure that the onions fry properly but do not burn. Remove the pan from the stove at any sign of this happening. Lift the onion flakes out with a pancake turner and drain thoroughly on paper toweling.

When onion flakes of either sort are cool and dry, they can be stored in a screw-top jar for use later. Be careful not to salt them before doing this, however, or they will go soft. Salt the portion required just before using.

NOTES ON VEGETABLES IN SOUTH EAST ASIAN FOOD

One of the greatest virtues of South East Asian food is that, as in Chinese cooking, the vegetables used emerge crunchy and with their vitamins not lost through over-cooking. You will often find in these recipes an instruction such as 'simmer (or stir-fry) until the vegetables are cooked but not soft.' This means that they should have absorbed some of the juice of the dish but should still retain their crisp texture.

Many of the recipes talk about forming chillies and radishes into flower shapes for garnish. This is how you do it:

Chillies. First push a sharp needle through the chilli about ½ inch from the stem, and pull it along sideways to the other end of the fruit so that the chilli is now bisected except at its stem end. Remove the seeds and core, then repeat the process with the needle until there are 6 or 8 'petals.' Now soak the chilli in iced water and the 'petals' will curl up.

Radishes. Treat long radishes in the same way using a sharp knife instead of a needle. There is, of course, no core to be removed in a radish. With small round radishes cut about 5 thin slices part of the way into the flesh around their circumference. They can then be soaked in the same way.

HOW TO CHOOSE AND PREPARE CHICKENS
FOR DIFFERENT PURPOSES

It is better always to choose roasting or frying chickens for Asian food. This is certainly so for Chinese cooking, where nothing remains on the fire for very long. But it is generally the case with curries as well. Though you can sometimes leave curried dishes to simmer until the meat is tender, your concentration is often caught up in achieving the right thickness of the gravy. For this reason I recommend sticking to roasters so that you can be fairly sure, no matter what, that your chicken will be tender enough.

The following ways to prepare a bird are referred to in this book:

Curry pieces. Disjoint the chicken in the normal way – legs in two, wings in two, breast in two lengthwise, back in two or three crosswise.

Frying pieces. This method usually applies in Chinese recipes. Since the purpose is to prepare pieces of chicken that can be handled with chopsticks, they are smaller than curry pieces.

First remove the legs and wings from the trunk at their connecting joints. Chop the wings again at each joint, and then across diagonally once between the joints. Spread the leg and thigh out to form a 'V' and chop diagonally across through the bone in about ¾-inch strips. Now take the trunk and chop it right through slightly to one side of the sternum and backbone to produce two halves, one slightly bigger than the other. Place each half face up on the chopping board, and chop diagonally all the way down so that you have a number of clean strips, about ¾ inch wide and 2 inches long, with bone, on which the meat has been cut across the grain. You can treat chickens this way before cooking, and you can also apply this method to chickens that have been steamed or roasted whole. In the latter case, it is usual then to arrange the pieces neatly on a serving dish in the shape of a spread out whole chicken.

Panggang preparation of chicken. Sever a whole chicken down the sternum only and bend it back flat, breaking the rib bones at the back to make this possible. Pin the legs down level with the tail by inserting a skewer across the back of the chicken. Keep the chicken flattened out as it cooks and serve whole in this way.

How to bone and shred a whole chicken. Cut the flesh of a whole chicken down each side of the breastbone and down the centre of the back and pull the flesh off half the bird at a time, releasing

24

the thigh, bone and all, from the body as you go. Remove the skin and quarter the body flesh. Bone and skin each wing and the leg. Dip the pieces of meat in water and cut across into thin escalopes. Finally chop these thin slices across the grain into long strips.

HOW TO MINCE AND SLICE FOR CHINESE COOKING

The most efficient way to mince meat or shrimp for Chinese cooking is to use two cleavers of equal weight, one in each hand. Chop down alternately on the ingredient being minced until it has become as fine as you need it. This may take a little practice for a while, but it will pay off in speed, cleanliness and lack of waste in the end.

To produce meat slices for Chinese cooking cut the whole chunk into 2-inch-by-2-inch strips first and then finally cut each piece into thin strips (about $\frac{1}{16}$ inch wide) across the grain.

HOW TO JUDGE AND MEASURE QUANTITIES
OF INGREDIENTS

Throughout this book I have tried to give exact quantities in my recipes. But the reader must recognize that these are only meant to be a guide. In fact, trying to estimate these quantities has been the hardest part of my task. South East Asian cooks seldom measure exactly when they are cooking. The Chinese vary quantities according to what is demanded by the situation of the moment. If they have a particularly honoured guest they will use more of the expensive ingredients; if they wish to save money they will use few of these. Indians and Malays tend to keep adding more of each ingredient until the dish tastes right, and look at you askance if you ask exactly how much of a particular spice went in. The quantities which I have set down are therefore those which in practice have seemed right to me: I have in each case tried to re-create the dish as I first met it in its own country. Nonetheless I fully expect other people to adapt my recipes according to their own tastes.

The lesson to be learned from all this is that it is not only permissible but also positively desirable to be relaxed as you proceed with Asian cooking. Never be overawed by a recipe, and never feel unable to adjust where adjustment suggests itself.

CONVENTIONS IN CURRY COOKING

Curries can end up being either 'wet' – that is, with lots of gravy, or 'dry' – that is, with little or no gravy at all. Those that aim to be dry usually require that the sauce be allowed to evaporate as the curry cooks. Sometimes it may do so completely, leaving behind a residue of oil in which the meat or vegetables that remain are allowed finally to fry, thus sealing in their juices.

Curries made with coconut milk are not usually covered as they cook. This not only prevents them from curdling but also allows for the dehydration, at least some of which is generally called for in South East Asian curries.

Many of the Indonesian and Malay recipes which follow talk about letting a dish simmer 'until the gravy has thickened and the oil has come out.' When you are cooking with coconut milk this unmistakably happens as the dish simmers unstirred and sufficient water evaporates out of the gravy. When this occurs the curry is neither really wet nor wholly dry: it is thick.

Curries are cooked on a *medium* heat.

WHERE TO SHOP FOR SOUTH EAST ASIAN INGREDIENTS

Many of the recipes in this book stipulate ingredients that are 'obtainable in Chinese shops.' There are usually two distinct kinds of food shops in the Chinese quarters of Western cities. They can be described as Chinese grocers and Chinese delicatessens. The first sell dried and canned goods and implements, the second smallgoods (fresh soya bean curd, Chinese sausages, fishballs, Sar Chiew meats) and Chinese fresh vegetables.

In many of the large cities of the United States, there is usually at least one Oriental or South East Asian grocery store which carries ingredients mentioned in this book. Many are even willing to fill mail orders.*

Across the country you can try the following stockists: in Boston, Sun Sun Company, 34a Oxford Street; in Chicago, Min Sun Trading Company, 2222–2228 South La Salle Street, and Man Sun Wing Company, 229 South Wentworth Avenue; in Dallas, Jung Oriental Foods and Gifts, 2519 North Fitzhugh; in Denver, Pacific Mercantile Company, 1946 Larimer Street; in Houston, Cheng Mee Company, 712 Franklin Street, and Great Oriental Import and Export, 2009 Polk Street; in Los Angeles, Yee Sing Chong Company, 960 Castelau Street, and Farmer's Market-Chinese Kitchen, West Third and Fairfax; in New York City, Eastern Trading Company, 2801 Broadway, Wing Fat Company, 33–35 Mott Street, The Java-India Company, 442 Hudson Street, and The Yuit Hing Market, 23 Pell Street; in Philadelphia, Wing On Grocery Store, 1005 Race Street; in San Francisco, Kwong Hang Company, 918 Grant Avenue, and Mow Lee Sing Kee Company, 730 Grant Avenue; and in Washington, D.C., New China Supply Company, 709 H Street, N.W., and Mee Wah Lung Company, 608 H Street, N.W. Almost all of these stores have daily supplies of perishable foods such as soya bean curd and bean sprouts, as well as the canned and dried ingredients.

Shops in the numerous Chinatowns across the country are no longer the only source for Chinese, Malay and Indian ingredients. These can be obtained in fancy-food stores, in gourmet departments of big city department stores, and even in local supermarkets.

---

* The best mail-order source for Indonesian and other South East Asian ingredients is Mrs. De Wildt, R.F.D. 1, Bangor, Pennsylvania. A free price list will be mailed to you upon request.

Ingredients

Bamboo shoots. The shoots of very young bamboos are collected before they appear above the ground. When used fresh they need to be boiled for a long time. Bamboo shoots are available already cooked and ready to use in many modern supermarkets as well as Chinese grocers. Slice across before adding to a dish.

Basil. Sweet basil has a green scented leaf that is also a favourite with Italians. It is quite easy to grow in rich soil with full sun. A few plants can be potted and brought indoors for winter use.

Bean sprouts or pea sprouts. These are large white shoots sprouted from soya beans, or smaller ones sprouted from a kind of Chinese pea and can be bought in cans or fresh, but the tinned variety should be strictly avoided. Patient and dedicated cooks pull off the skins of the peas or beans before adding these to a dish.

You can make your own pea sprouts by taking 1 lb. Chinese green peas (*lok doe* in Cantonese). Put them in a large bowl and cover them generously with cold water. When the skin has split (about 24 hours later), strain off the water through a colander. Leave the peas in this, covering them with a folded linen dish-towel. Water the whole thing every 2 or 3 hours for 3 days. The peas should remain wet, but should not rest in water or they will become brown and smelly. (Should this happen you will have to start again.)

After 3 days, when the sprouts themselves should look fresh and white, tip the contents of the colander into a large container, fill with water, and stir vigorously until the skins float on top. Repeat this process until as many skins as possible have floated off and been scooped out. The rest you will have to take off by hand.

Blachan or trasi. This is a basic flavouring all over South East Asia. It is made from prawns or shrimps, salted, dried, pounded and rotted, then formed into cakes. It can be either pink, soft and mushy, or darker in colour and hard. In one form or the other it is usually available either in packages or cans. As it is very strong smelling once opened it should be transferred to a jar or plastic box with a tight fitting lid and kept in the refrigerator. Blachan should always be fried before it is used. If you are frying all the spices, just add it as one of them. If you are not frying the others, wrap the blachan in foil and roast it in a pan on top of the stove for a minute or two. Remove the foil wrapper (which will have prevented the smell from penetrating the house) and grind the roasted blachan with the other spices. If blachan is not available you can use shrimp paste or anchovy paste. When my recipes suggest a 'slice' of hard trasi, it signifies a cut $\frac{1}{8}$ inch thick. 'A square inch slice of trasi,' then, measures 1 inch by 1 inch by $\frac{1}{8}$ inch approximately.

Cardamom. A strongly scented, slightly bitter Indian spice, cardamom is best bought whole in its green or white fibre pods, which are about the size of a little fingernail. Roughly break these open before adding to a dish. Each pod contains 6–8 individual seeds. I have usually mentioned only the number of pods that are to be added in the recipes in this book. If you have cardamom seeds, not pods, remember the equivalents.

Celery. The celery that is used in South East Asia is never allowed to grow to the large size that we know – it looks more like thick stalks of parsley. It is used as a garnish, not as a vegetable. If you are using the large, coarse variety, you should take only the smaller leafy end of each stalk. I am told by an Indonesian friend with a German neighbour that the above-ground leaves and stalks of the root vegetable celeriac are even more appropriate.

Chillies. There are many varieties of this delectable vegetable, ranging from that tiny ball of fire, the 'birdseye' chilli, to the insipid sweet capsicum, or bell pepper, of the United States. Those used in South East Asia are the smaller, hotter ones – either the 'birdseye' (about $\frac{1}{2}$ inch long) or a medium one (about

2 or 3 inches). The largest are no more than 4 or 5 inches long and are still narrow. The chillies to be used can be either green or red, fresh or dried. I have usually stipulated which in these recipes. If fresh chillies are listed in the ingredients of a recipe but are not available, use Conimex or other brand 'Sambal Oelek' from the jar. This is simply a preparation of fresh hot chillies crushed with salt. 1 teaspoon = about 2 hot chillies.

People who have not cooked with hot chillies before should be warned that they are extremely savage unless one is used to them. *Don't* take a large bite of a raw chilli to try it out: a careful nibble might even prove more than you bargained for. And wash your hands carefully after cutting them as the juice should not be allowed to come into contact with your eyes or your baby's skin.

Chillies, as this suggests, have not so much a taste as a chemical effect. This effect may have to be tolerated rather than enjoyed to begin with, but once the initial shock has passed you will find that chillies in food tend to stimulate the appetite, cool the body temperature, and bring about a general feeling of peace and benignity. When you have become an admirer it is difficult to resist moving on to addiction.

Chinese cabbage. There are two main types of Chinese cabbage – bitter Chinese cabbage (*kai choy*), sometimes known as Chinese mustard greens, which has pale green stems and leaves, and *bak choy*, sometimes known as Chinese green cabbage, with smooth white stems and dark green leaves. The former tastes rather like Belgian endive, the latter is the colour of Swiss chard. There is a third variety with a wide rippled stem that is called in English 'celery cabbage.'

When a recipe specifies simply 'Chinese cabbage,' either of the latter two will do – or even chard, or celery – but when it says 'bitter Chinese cabbage' or 'kai choy' you must use either that or Belgian endive.

Chinese mushrooms. These are dried whole mushrooms and rather expensive, but, since they are very strong-tasting, you usually need only a few. Chinese mushrooms give a distinctive flavour to the dishes which contain them, so when they are called for it will not do to substitute either fresh or canned mushrooms. Nor would European dried mushrooms be suitable. Chinese dried mushrooms are readily available in Chinese groceries. To cook them, soak them in warm water until soft, remove the hard stems, and slice or use whole.

Chinese vermicelli. Called *fun see* in Cantonese, this is a fine, clear type of noodle made from pea starch (see also *Noodles*, below).

Cinnamon bark. In South East Asia this comes in strips about $\frac{1}{16}$ inch thick. In Western countries it tends to be more finely flaked. Allow for the difference when following the measurements here. A '1-inch' piece of cinnamon bark means a collection of pieces which if put together would measure about 1 inch in length and $\frac{1}{16}$ inch in thickness.

Citrus leaves. These are often added to curries for flavouring. Lemon or lime leaves are best.

Cloud ear or tree fungus or jelly mushroom. This Chinese vegetable is black and hard in its dried form, and its common English name is quite descriptive. When soaked in water it becomes soft and jelly-like.

Cloves. Few people will be unacquainted with this spice as it has been used for flavouring in our world since the discovery of the Spice Islands.

Coconut milk. See p. 21.

Coconut oil. For dishes in which you go on to use coconut milk this is the usual frying medium. Coconut oil can be bought in solid form, though the liquid would be more appropriate for dishes that are to be allowed to cool. In the absence of liquid coconut oil use peanut oil.

Coriander. The seed is a basic ingredient of all South East Asian curries. It is better to buy all dry spices as seeds and grind them yourself, in order to be sure of their freshness.

The root is a uniquely Thai contribution to South East Asian food. It is used crushed with garlic to flavour meat and it also makes something specifically local out of curries introduced from India and soups derived from Chinese recipes.

The leaves are used as a garnish in both Thailand and Malaya. Though they look something like parsley and are often called 'Thai parsley' or 'Chinese parsley,' their flavour is unmistakably different, being rather strong and not always acceptable to the foreign palate. So universal and inevitable is it to find Thai dishes garnished with these leaves that even more Thais can be irritated by the habit. One nobleman recently was seen to be rather upset when on a dinner table everything was covered with them, and said to his host, 'I like it, but for goodness' sake don't spoil everything with it.'

Coriander root and coriander leaves are not generally easy to buy, but they grow quickly from seeds planted in spring and summer. Make sure that the plants are well protected, however, as snails love them. The coriander seeds which you buy as a spice are suitable for planting.

Cumin seed. What I have said about coriander seed applies also to cumin. When the Malay terms are literally translated, it is the 'white cumin' that is cumin as we know it. 'Sweet cumin' is really fennel seed.

Curry leaves. These are used as a flavouring throughout South East Asia. They are readily available packaged in dried form. I have become firmly convinced in my own mind that these are identical with the Indonesian *salaam*, though they appear smaller and finer than the latter when fresh. If they are not the same, they are certainly closer than any other substitute that is ever recommended.

Fennel seeds. These are the same shape as cumin seeds, only larger and whiter in colour. Because of this, and because their

Malay name is translatable as 'sweet cumin,' the two are often confused. Fennel seeds have an aniseed flavour.

Fenugreek. Yellowish, small and oblong in shape, this Indian seed is used in small quantities in some Indian curry powders. It is the ingredient which gives the characteristic bland smell to old-fashioned European commercial curry powders, in which I feel it is over-emphasized.

Fish sauce. This is a dark flavouring agent used in Thai food. It resembles light soya sauce which may be used in its place, although it is readily available at Chinese grocers.

Garlic. The South East Asian variety of garlic is much the same as the English and American, only the individual cloves are often smaller and a whole bulb will contain no more than four or five. To prepare garlic for curries, peel the cloves, smash them with the flat side of a cleaver, and chop roughly with the blunt edge. This method gives more aromatic results than a garlic squeezer, and you still avoid getting the smell on your hands.

Ghee. This is clarified butter. It can usually be bought in Indian groceries.

Green ginger. The root of the ginger plant, which is of Indian or Chinese origin, is used all over South East Asia. For cooking it must always be fresh (not powdered) and young. When you acquire ginger root in that part of the world it is tender and juicy, whereas the roots we buy are almost always old and fibrous. When I speak of a 'slice' of green ginger in this book I mean an average cross-section. There is no need to worry about whether you are cutting from the thin part or the thick part of the irregular root. To prepare green ginger for curries, proceed in the same way as for garlic.

Ginger juice comes from very fresh young ginger smashed and squeezed. It can also be obtained from old pieces that have been moistened in warm water.

Green gram. This is a kind of dried pea known throughout the area and used for many things – from pea sprouts and Chinese vermicelli to Indian and Malay sweets.

Green onions. These are small white onions with green leaves, all of which are used.

Kentjur. This root has a flavour a little like camphor. I do not know how to translate it into English, but its botanical name is *Kaempferia pandurata.* Conimex now supply it in dried form, but it can be left out of recipes without great harm.

Laos or lengkuas or Java root. This is another root that looks rather like ginger. It is, however, more medicinal in flavour. It grows throughout South East Asia and there it is used fresh, but so far only dried and powdered laos can be bought in Europe, America and Australia. It is distributed by Conimex, a Dutch condiment firm which exports to the United States. One slice of fresh laos, usually about $\frac{1}{8}$ inch thick, equals $\frac{1}{2}$ teaspoon of laos powder.

Lemon grass. If you can obtain a root of this beautifully aromatic tropical grass you should be able to get it to grow in your garden. Once established, it multiplies easily in most places in the summer months. During the winter in frosty areas it should be lifted out of the ground, potted and kept alive indoors. A 'stalk' of lemon grass signifies a whole stem, which is round and close packed like that of a very small leek. Conimex sell dried, powdered lemon grass. They call it 'Sereh Powder.' One teaspoon of this would equal about 1 stalk of fresh lemon grass. If you cannot get lemon grass in any form, use a strip of thinly pared lemon peel instead.

Lentil. There are many kinds of lentil employed in Indian cooking, especially in the south where meat is not eaten. The most common are the yellow split pea (*chenna* or *chanai*), red Egyptian lentils (*masoor* or *Mysore dhall*) or the flat black or green lentils.

Lily buds, dried. These are available in Chinese groceries.

Macadamia nuts. These are very nearly if not exactly the same as *kemiri* or *buah kras.* They are sometimes known as popple nuts and are used raw in cooking except where otherwise specified. In this state they taste quite tart and not altogether pleasant in themselves. If Macadamia nuts are not available, substitute blanched almonds. Indonesians and Malays themselves often prefer the latter where they are available.

Monosodium glutamate. This is known throughout the world under various names: Ve-Tsin, Ajinomoto, Mei Ching, Taste Powder, Gourmet Powder, P'sst!, Accent, etc. Use sparingly in Chinese cooking and only when you are economizing on ingredients that create their own broth (e.g. meats).

Mustard seed. This is much used in South Indian and Ceylon cooking. The whole seeds are usually dry-fried before being ground for curry powder. When added to food on their own they are not finely ground but roughly broken instead.

Noodles. This usually signifies Chinese dried wheat-flour noodles when not called vermicelli.

Nutmeg. This spice is so well known that it needs no comment, except to say that a whole nutmeg grated when needed produces a better flavour than ready ground nutmeg.

Onions. In South East Asian food small Bombay onions, or red onions, and not large Spanish onions are the ones mostly used. These are drier and easier to slice and grind than our or your common yellow-skinned onions. They are sometimes available to us under the name of shallots but they are not often to be found in shops. (You can order shallots by mail from Les Eschalottes, Ramsey, New Jersey.) I have used the brown Spanish onion in these recipes, but choose Bombays if at all possible. One Spanish onion = 4 Bombay onions or shallots.

Before adding chopped Spanish onions to a spices paste for frying always squeeze out as much excess moisture as possible. If the mixture is too wet, the spices will stew rather than fry.

Peanuts in sauces. Many Malay and Indonesian recipes include a sauce using ground peanuts. It is best to buy raw peanuts to be dry-fried and then crushed for this purpose. However, to save time you can use crunchy peanut butter in equal amounts, but be warned that this never tastes exactly the same.

Pepper. This can be either black or white pepper, but it should always be freshly ground.

Sesame oil. Bottles of this can be bought from Chinese or Japanese grocers. It is expensive and concentrated and is used as a flavouring in Chinese food, not as a frying medium.

Shrimp, *dried.* These are prawns or shrimps that have been dried in the sun and are available in Chinese shops under the name *har mei.*

Soya bean curd. A soft, white, cheese-like cake, this is used extensively in Chinese and Malay cooking. It is available fresh in Chinese delicatessens and also in cans. Dried bean curd, used only in Chinese cooking, comes in flat sheets or in twists.

Soya sauce. Three kinds of soya sauce are used in this book. They are light soya sauce and dark soya sauce (which is thicker and heavier), both of which are obtainable at Chinese grocers, and also Javanese soya sauce, which is sweet and very thick. This last is sometimes available in bottles called Ketjab Manis, or Ketjap Benteng, under the label of Conimex. You can make it yourself, however, according to the following recipe:

Javanese Soya Sauce

1 cup dark soya sauce
½ cup molasses
3 tablespoons brown sugar

Combine all ingredients in a small saucepan over a medium heat. Stir until the sugar melts. Keep in a covered jar.

Star anise. The dried spice both looks and tastes as it sounds. Imagine a brown dried apple core cut into a cross section with seeds. This is just what star anise looks like only it is larger. A 'point' of star anise includes both seed case and seed.

Tamarind. People who live on a diet high in carbohydrates value tamarind for its laxative properties. It is a ripened fibrous pod which is generally used in curries for its acidic effect. Tomatoes, lemon juice or vinegar will do just as well. Tamarind pulp can be bought in bags in Chinese shops and in many fancy-food stores. It is usually added to cooking in the form of tamarind water.

To make this, soak, for example, a walnut-sized piece of tamarind pulp in $\frac{1}{2}$ cup warm water until soft. Squeeze out repeatedly and discard the fibrous material, using the liquid that is left.

Turmeric. Mistakenly translated as 'saffron' in Ceylon, turmeric is really a yellow root resembling ginger, only smaller. It is used fresh in Indonesia and Malaya, though we know it in the West only in its dried and powdered form.

Water chestnut. This is a Chinese vegetable notable for its crisp texture. It is available in cans in Chinese groceries and most modern supermarkets.

Glossary

English	Indonesian	Malay	Indian (Hindustani and Tamil)	Chinese (Cantonese)	Thai
bamboo shoot	rebung	rebung	—	dung shung	nor my
basil	kemangi	kemangi selaseh	—	—	horapa
bean sprouts or pea sprouts	taoge	taugeh	—	ngah choy	thua ngork
blachan	trasi, blatjan	blachan	blachang	—	kapi
cardamom	kapulaga	buah pelaga	elachi or elam	—	grawahn, kravan
celery	seledri, seldri	daun seladri	—	—	pak chi farang
chillies	lombok, tjabé	chabai	mirchi or mooloogah	fan chiew	prik ki nu, prik ki fah
cinnamon bark	kaju manis, manis djangan	kayu manis	dhall cheene, karuvappadai	—	op chery
citrus leaves	djeruk perut	limau purut	—	—	makrut bai
cloud ear or tree fungus	kuping djamu	kuping tikus	—	wung yee	hed hunu
cloves	tjengkeh	bunga chingkek	laong or lavungam	—	gahn plu
coconut milk	santan kental (thick), santan	santan	nariyal ka dhud or thengai pal	—	hua kathi (thick), hang kathi (thin)

'—' indicates that the item is not commonly used in the country's cooking

coriander seed	ketumbar	ketumbar	dhuniah or kothamilee	—	pak chi met
root	—	—	—	—	pak chi rahk
leaf	daun ketumbar	daun ketumbar	—	—	pak chi bai
cumin seed	djinten	jintan puteh	suduru (Sinhalese), jeera or cheeregum	—	yira
curry leaves	daun salaam	—	karapincha or karupillay	—	—
Chinese vermicelli	so'on, laksa	laksa, beehoon	—	fun see	wun sen
dried bean curd	—	—	—	fooh jook	forng tawhu
dried prawns or shrimp	udang kering	udang kering	—	haah mei	kung haeng
fennel	adas	jintan manis	saunf or vendhyam, mahaduru (Sinhalese)	—	yira
fenugreek	—	—	methee or ventayam	—	—
fish sauce	—	—	—	yu chiap	nam plah
garlic	bawang puteh	bawang puteh	lusson or vellay poondoo	suen tau	krathiem
green ginger	djahe, aliah	halia	udruk or ingee	sang keong	king
green gram	katjang hidjau	kachang hijau	dhall	lok doe	thua khiaw, thua thorng
green onions	daun bawang	daun bawang	—	choong	ton horm

'—' indicates that the item is not commonly used in the country's cooking

Glossary *cntd.*

English	Indonesian	Malay	Indian (Hindustani and Tamil)	Chinese (Cantonese)	Thai
kentjur	kentjur	kunchor	—	—	krachai
laos (galangal)	laos, lengkuas	langkuas	—	—	kah
lemon grass	seré	serai	sera (Sinhalese)	—	takrai
lemon or lime	djeruk nipis	limau nipis	nimbu or yellumshikai	—	makrut
Macadamia nut	kemiri	buah kras	—	—	—
mustard seed	—	biji sawi	rai or kudoo	—	—
noodles (wheat)	mie	mee	—	mien	bamee
nutmeg	pala	buah pala	jaiphul or jathikka	—	look jun
onions (red or Bombay)	bawang merah	bawang merah	peaz or vunguim	—	hua horm
peanuts	katjang tanah	kachang tanah	—	fah sang	thua lisong
pepper	meritja, lada	lada	kala mirchi or moloo	—	prik Thai
soya bean curd	tahu	tauhu	—	tow fu	taw hu
soya sauce (dark)	ketjap	kichup, tauyu	—	see you	nam pla siiw
soya sauce (light)	—	—	—	sung chow	nam pla siiw
star anise	bunga lawang	bunga lawang	—	pak kok or peh kah	—
tamarind	asam Djawa	asam	imlee or pulee	—	makahm
turmeric	kunjit	kunyit	huldee or munjal	—	kamin
water chestnut	—	mah tai	—	ma tai	gajup

'—' indicates that the item is not commonly used in the country's cooking

Indonesia

'SELAMAT MAKAN!' ('Good eating!') is the ritual toast at the beginning of a meal in Indonesia.

Indonesian food, with its variety of taste and texture and an accompanying grace of presentation, has always made eating an event of great joy in that country. This is so, as Stamford Raffles observed, for the foreigner as much as for the family. In his *History of Java*, published in 1817, he remarked:

By the custom of the country, good food and lodging are ordered to be provided for all strangers and travellers arriving at a village; and in no country are the rights of hospitality more strictly enjoined by institutions, or more conscientiously and religiously observed by custom and practice. 'It is not sufficient,' say the Javan institutions, 'that a man should place good food before his guest; he is bound to do more: he should render the meal palatable by kind words and treatment, to soothe him after his journey, and to make his heart glad while he partakes of the refreshment.' This is called *bojo kromo*, or real hospitality.

That was 150 years ago; and we may well not be able to attain this matchless ideal of *bojo kromo* in the fast and furious world of the present. We should, however, be able at least to approach it.

To be sure, the quite ordinarily equipped urban Indonesian kitchen even today embraces at least one domestic servant – a rare commodity in European countries or the United States. Yet all that is really needed to make a start in the direction of good Indonesian food is a little care on the part of the cook, some patience, and a sensitivity to the potentialities of her gas or electric stove.

Interest in the outcome is the first qualification, and nothing will stimulate this more quickly than the tantalizing smells that issue from the cooking area as those marvellous spices begin to spatter in the pan.

The most important of these are hot chilli (both the medium length one – *tjabé* – and the very small green or red 'birdseye' chilli – *lombok*), trasi or blachan, laos or lengkuas, salaam or curry leaves, serai or lemon grass, turmeric, coriander, cumin, garlic and onions (preferably Bombay onions or shallots), coconut milk, tamarind, limes or lemon juice, green ginger, basil and citrus leaves. Occurring in other recipes are the 'dry' spices – nutmeg, cloves, cinnamon and fennel. I have discussed all of these spices in my preceding chapter; and you should not find it difficult to obtain them in any large city.

The Indonesia of today is a country of great variety – in agriculture, in experience of and contact with the outside world, in social patterns, and in religious and cultural expression. It is nothing if not heterogeneous. At different periods of its history it has been influenced by India (both Hindu-Buddhist and Moslem), by Arab traders and scholars, by trading and immigrant Chinese, and by the Dutch. All these influences manifest themselves in some startlingly different ways in various parts of the country. And all of them are reflected truthfully in the food of the different areas. In recipes from Atjeh and North Sumatra, where Islam first took root in the archipelago, you find an obvious use of Indian and Arab spices: ginger and pepper, cinnamon, cardamom and fennel. In Central Sumatra and Minangkabau, where greater agricultural wealth tends to combine with scholasticism and religious orthodoxy, food is prepared from solid raw materials in a rather austere fashion. Meat and fish dishes prevail. Central Java is the land of intensive rice agriculture, of deep tradition, of pomp and conspicuous consumption as well as universal poverty, and its religion is tinged with animism. Here there is a particular emphasis on artistic, light-handed, festival-type foods. Vegetables are used more often than meat. West Java or Sunda is perhaps the most interesting of all. This area has been close to the inland Central Javanese world but has known in its past religious and economic affinity to parts of Sumatra. Sundanese cuisine combines both Javanese sophistication and lightness with Sumatran abundance and solidity.

Encompassing this variety, one can say of Indonesian food that it is inclined to follow one of two tendencies. The first is the style of what a sociologist might call 'interior' agricultural

42

societies; the second that of more outward-oriented trading and coastal ones. In the former, not only culinary but also social and economic influences that come from outside tend to be absorbed and modified in the light of local practice. They usually either fail or prevail according to whether the tradition they encounter is in sympathy with them or not. Whichever happens, it is the local tradition that determines the course of events. In the trade-lands, however, things tend to occur the other way around: outside influences in food as well as culture play a determining role.

In this chapter I have vastly oversimplified this picture by describing the first as 'Javanese,' the second as 'Sumatran.' Of course there are 'interior' cultures (like that of the Karo Bataks) in Sumatra, and outward-oriented pockets (like Bantam, West Java) in Java. But I have found that, overall, the distinction is useful in helping people to develop an understanding of Indonesian food. What is said generally about the tendencies in Sumatran food can also be applied to the food of the other 'Outer Islands' of the Indonesian archipelago. I include no specific examples, however, since I have not been able to collect recipes in these areas.

In 'interior' societies you tend to get simple basic materials, sometimes arranged in a sophisticated fashion. You find fresh spices used to flavour cooking. Recipes from Java, for instance, use lots of sugar, which grows there. They also feature laos or Java root, a root typical of the padi areas of South East Asia, and trasi or shrimp paste, a processed sea-food, both of which are important ingredients of Thai cooking. This is significant because Thailand can also be described as having a similar 'interior' culture.

Sumatrans, on the other hand, use ginger, a plant of foreign origin, as much as or more than laos. They are fonder of chillies which come originally from elsewhere. They use neither trasi nor sugar. The spices on which trade is built are more often blended for flavouring a single, solid, main ingredient. This, I suggest, is the pattern of outward-oriented cultures. It is therefore not surprising that it should also be evident in the Malay recipes which appear later in this book.

If a cook wishes to specialize in a particular cuisine, the more background knowledge she has the better. She is then able to see individual dishes and whole menus in their proper cultural and culinary context. The beginner, however, should not be daunted. All you need to start with is a collection of recipes and a list of suggested menus (I give some later in this introduction). But the cook who wishes to conquer with the variety of her dishes, the contrasts of their textures, the subtlety with which their flavours are blended, and the beauty of their appearance, must go further. It is as important for her to know something about the possibilities of a recipe from a certain area as it is for her to have the good sense to ensure that each dish she serves within a meal possesses a different basic ingredient.

There is one final pointer to the art of planning good Indonesian menus. That is to note what is implied by the name of any particular dish. You will see that in most subsections that follow there are recipes having the same general name as others elsewhere which use a different basic ingredient. For example, there is Sambal Goreng Sajuran and Sambal Goreng Hati; Ajam Semur Djawa and Ikan Semur Djawa; Rudjak and Ajam Bumbu Rudjak. All dishes with the same general name are either flavoured with a similar blend of spices or cooked in a similar fashion. A rough list of general headings would include Dadar (omelette), Sambal Goreng (something chilli-fried), Semur ('Smoor'), Panggang (barbecued or broiled), Gulé (curry), Pangé (sour stew), Atjar (pickle), Bumbu Rudjak ('Rudjak' spices), Bumbu Ketjap (spices with soya sauce), Bumbu Padang ('Padang' spices), Kormah ('Korma'), Sajur (vegetables in broth).

To construct a properly balanced Indonesian meal, then, you should start with a basis of rice (usually plain) and a sambal, and add upwards of four other dishes chosen with a mind to basic ingredient (soup, fish, chicken, meat, vegetable or egg), place of origin, and style of cooking and flavouring.

To begin with, here are some suggested menus. Once you have mastered these, you should feel free to branch out on your own. 'Selamat Makan!'

Menus

I

White Rice
Sambal Goreng Udang
Opor Ajam
Sajur Lodeh
Krupuk

II

White Rice
Gulé Kambing
Atjar Tjampur
Saté Ketjap
Sajur Bajam
Krupuk

III

White Rice
Ajam Goreng
Karé Djawa
Petjel
Sajur Asam

IV

White Rice
Rendang
Gado-Gado
Ikan Semur *or* Ajam
    Semur Djawa
Krupuk

V

White Rice
Atjar Ikan
Ajam Panggang
Sambal Goreng Telor
Sajur Bobor
Krupuk

VI

White Rice
Saté Ajam
Sambal Goreng Hati
Rudjak
Sajur Karé
Krupuk

VII

White Rice
Singgang Ajam
Gulé Udang
Tahu Goreng Ketjap
Sajur Asam
Krupuk

VIII

White Rice
Ajam Bumbu Rudjak
Abon
Tumis
Sajur Lemeng
Krupuk

IX	X
White Rice	White Rice
Lapis Daging **Semarang**	Gulé Masin Ikan
Gulé Ajam	Magbub *or* Daging
Bégedel Djagung	Masak Bali
Sajur Bajam	Asinan
Krupuk	Sajur Terung
	Krupuk

For a celebration, you can serve a special rice dish, a *soto* (see pp. 52-9), and up to a dozen other dishes including fish, poultry, beef,. mutton, a cooked mixed vegetable dish, a salad, sambal goreng, some preserved sambals, patties, and krupuk (see p. 116). This would of course be the sort of occasion when there would be more than one cook.

Special Rice Dishes and Noodles

NASI GURIH (Coconut Rice)

Nasi Gurih is a basic rice dish which appears on many festive occasions – both family ones and religious.

2 cups long-grain white rice
1 curry leaf
1-inch-stem lemon grass, bruised, *or* 1 teaspoon grated lemon or lime
    peel
3 cups medium-thick coconut milk
salt to taste

Thoroughly wash the rice in a strainer until the water that pours through it emerges *quite* clear. Combine coconut milk, salt, curry leaf and lemon grass in a saucepan with a tight fitting lid and bring to the boil. Put in the rice and proceed to cook it in the coconut liquid in the normal way according to the evaporation method (see p. 20).

Nasi Gurih is served differently according to the occasion. At a wedding feast it would be presented accompanied by the traditional wedding side dishes of the area – in Central Java perhaps Saté Bandeng, Ajam Panggang, Telor Asin (a salty egg dish not included here), Sambal Goreng Sajuran, Urap, Atjar Ketimun; in Sumatra, say, Sambal Goreng Hati, Bégedel Kentang with a garnish of Serundeng, Singgang Ajam, Atjar Kuning, and one or two other substantial dishes according to the host's purse.

Two calendrical festivals – *Muludan* (the Birth of the Prophet) and *Maleman* (the evening festival held during the fast month) often feature Nasi Gurih served with accompanying dishes which together make up a meal known as Nasi Wuduk. It consists of Nasi Gurih arranged in a wide circle around the edge of a plate with Opor Ajam placed in the centre. The whole dish is then decorated with basil leaves, chopped celery and cucumber slices and garnished with the crisp-fried pork rinds that can be bought in bags. (Indonesians, of course, being Moslems, use fried ox-skin rather than pork.) It is accompanied by a separate plate of Sambal Goreng Udang, some preserved sambals, and a bowl of roasted peanuts.

NASI KUNING (Yellow Rice)

This is another way rice is cooked for festive occasions. The traditional foods served at the *Bruwah slametan* (the Breaking of the Fast) include Nasi Kuning and an Indonesian omelette. Both can be combined in a special garnished Nasi Kuning for parties.

To cook the rice

Wash white rice thoroughly until the water is completely clear. Half cook it in the usual way (that is, cook until the water is absorbed and then remove from the fire). In the meantime for each pound of rice put $2\frac{1}{2}$ cups thick coconut milk, $1\frac{1}{2}$ teaspoons turmeric, 2 or 3 curry leaves, and $\frac{3}{4}$ teaspoon laos powder (optional) in a saucepan. Bring to the boil and put in the half-cooked rice. Cook, uncovered, on an asbestos mat over a low flame for about another 30 minutes until the liquid has evaporated entirely and the steam is escaping through holes in the surface of the rice.

To serve

Heap the yellow rice on to a flat plate and scatter or arrange over the top a thin plain omelette sliced into 2-inch by $\frac{1}{4}$-inch strips, some basil leaves, fried onion flakes (see p. 22), sliced fresh red chilli, serundeng (see p. 115), and some very small balls of rempah (see p. 113) *or* fine slices of roast chicken meat. Arrange krupuk (see p. 116) or shrimp slices around the edge of the plate and serve.

NASI KEBULI (Indian Rice)

2 cups long-grain rice
1 young chicken
1 yellow onion, finely chopped
3 cloves garlic, smashed and chopped
1 tablespoon coriander
¾ teaspoon cumin seeds
¾ teaspoon laos powder *or* ¼-inch-slice green ginger
1-inch-stalk lemon grass, bruised
1-inch-piece cinnamon stick
a pinch of nutmeg
2 cloves
4 tablespoons butter or ghee

Grind the coriander and cumin to a powder in a blender. Tie the lemon grass, cinnamon and cloves in a muslin bag. Cut the chicken into serving pieces. Cover it with 3 cups water, put in the onion, garlic, and all the spices, bring to the boil and simmer until tender. Remove the chicken pieces while still hot and allow to drain and dry.

Meanwhile wash the rice in the usual way and soak it in water for about 1 hour. Drain it. Heat 4 tablespoons butter or ghee in a saucepan and fry the rice until it is transparent and yellow looking. Add 2 cups of the spiced chicken broth and boil until *all* the liquid has evaporated. Now turn the heat down to the lowest possible point, cover the saucepan, put an asbestos mat under it, and allow the rice to steam quietly for another 20 or 30 minutes until it is dry but tender.

Heat some more ghee and fry the chicken pieces until they are golden brown. Heap the rice on a plate, garnish with fried onion flakes and chopped basil or celery tops. Arrange the fried chicken around the edge and serve.

NASI GORENG (Fried Rice)

2 cups cold cooked rice
$\frac{1}{2}$ lb. shredded raw rump steak
a few shrimp, preferably raw, peeled and deveined (optional)
2 fresh red chillies
1 yellow onion
1 clove garlic
$\frac{3}{4}$ teaspoon trasi (blachan or shrimp paste) *or* $\frac{1}{2}$-inch-slice hard trasi salt
1 tablespoon dark soya sauce *or* Javanese soya sauce (see p. 36)
2 eggs
peanut oil

Beat the eggs with a pinch of salt. Heat 1 tablespoon oil in a pan, pour in the eggs, and cook as a thin omelette. Lift out and cut into 2-inch by $\frac{1}{4}$-inch strips. Leave aside. Grind the onion, chillies, garlic and trasi together. Heat 2 tablespoons oil in a wok or a pan and fry the spices until soft. Add the beef and shrimp and stir-fry until they are cooked, Put in the rice and mix everything thoroughly. Add more oil, if necessary, and the soya sauce, and keep stirring until the rice grains are well coated and the colour is even. Lift out on to a plate, garnish with shredded omelette, fried onion flakes (see p. 22), diced cucumber with its skin or chopped celery. In Indonesia, Nasi Goreng is usually served accompanied by fried eggs with a moist yolk and sliced sweet tomatoes.

BAHMIE GORENG (Fried Noodles) (Indonesian Chinese)

$\frac{1}{2}$ lb. Chinese wheat-noodles
1 large yellow onion
2 cloves garlic
meat from $\frac{1}{2}$ chicken, raw or cooked
$\frac{1}{8}$ lb. shrimp, raw or cooked (optional)
1 or 2 cabbage leaves
1 stalk clery, chopped
3 or 4 green onions with green leaves, chopped

1 tablespoon lard *or* 5 tablespoons coconut or peanut oil
1 cup chicken stock or bouillon
light soya sauce to taste
fresh chillies to taste

Cook the noodles as shown on the package. Then drain thoroughly and keep warm. Finely slice the onion and one clove garlic lengthwise. Heat the oil in a wok or a pan and when it is hot fry them until they are brown and crisp. Drain and dry on paper toweling, and keep aside. Bone and shred the chicken meat.Clean, shell and devein the shrimp, and finely shred the cabbage. Smash and roughly chop the remaining clove of garlic. Reheat 4 tablespoons oil in the wok and add the garlic. When it is soft put in the chicken meat and prawns, if these are not already cooked. (If you use cooked meat, add after the noodles.) Stir-fry until they change colour, then add the cabbage and stir-fry until this is cooked but not soft. Now add the cooked noodles. Stir thoroughly and fry until the noodles are coated with oil and the other ingredients well mixed. Finally add the stock and salt and pepper to taste. Lift from the fire and stir in light soya sauce to taste.

Dish out into a large shallow bowl. Garnish with the fried onion and garlic flakes, the chopped celery and the spring onions. Scatter over a few 'birdseye' chillies if you are an addict, or a sliced larger fresh chilli if you are more cautious, and serve.

Soups

Indonesian soups are not really what we understand soups to be. They take one of two forms. They may be substantial meat-broth dishes which are served either on their own with rice, as main dishes amongst others, or as rather special between-meal snacks. This is the type of dish known as *soto*. Or they may be the vegetable dishes with a coconut milk stock called *sajur-sajuran*. In either case they do not precede the rest of the meal as our soups do, but are served along with everything else. You allow the broth to moisten the rice on your plate and eat the meat or vegetable with the rice.

Whatever the *correct* practice may be, substantial mixtures of this sort are particularly well suited to informal use in families like mine where thick soups plus salad take the centre of the stage on Saturday or Sunday night.

SOTO AJAM

There are as many versions of Soto Ajam as there are cooks in Indonesia. The next four recipes represent only a sample. Sotos can actually be quite dressed-up meals in themselves. My first is presented in this way. The others can be served alone as a rather special soup course, or with rice as one of many main dishes.

I. NASI SOTO AJAM (Chicken Soup with Rice)

1 plump young hen
a dash of freshly ground black pepper
1½ teaspoons turmeric
3 Macadamia nuts
1 yellow onion
½-inch-slice green ginger
salt to taste
a little coconut or peanut oil

Clean and wash the fowl. Cover it with water and add salt to taste. Crush the nuts, smash and chop the ginger, chop the onion. Heat a little oil in a pan and fry the nuts and ginger until they are brown. Add these, the onion, pepper and turmeric to the chicken and simmer until it is tender. Lift the cooked whole chicken from the pot, drain it, and fry it in a little hot oil, turning frequently until it is brown. Cut the meat off the carcass, shred it, and keep it warm. Discard the carcass. Pour the soup into a large serving bowl and keep warm.

Accompaniments

As well as the meat and broth, have ready the following:

a large bowl of boiled rice
1 package of roughly broken potato chips
3 sliced hard-boiled eggs
½ lb. scalded bean sprouts
¼ cabbage shredded and lightly cooked
⅔ cup Chinese vermicelli soaked in water until soft, then fried
 for a minute in oil

Arrange these all on separate plates or decoratively in separate heaps on a large serving platter.

Garnishes

On another plate arrange the following garnishes:

finely chopped young celery
about 4 tablespoons crisply fried onion flakes
lemon wedges

Sambal

Prepare a sambal to be placed on the table by mincing a number of fresh red chillies to taste with 1-inch piece of green ginger. Moisten this with a dash of white vinegar and some of the chicken broth.

To serve Nasi Soto Ajam

The bowl of rice and the central soup bowl are placed on the table, surrounded by the plate of cooked vegetables, that of chicken meat, the plate of garnishes, and the sambal dish. Each person has his own plate in front of him, and helps himself to a portion of meat, hard-boiled egg slices, vegetables, potato chips and vermicelli – all piled on top of each other. The broth is then ladled over these, celery and onion flakes are sprinkled on, and lemon juice squeezed over to taste. Guests may serve themselves with rice in a separate bowl to eat with sambal alongside the soup, or they may add rice and sambal to their soup plate.

II. SOTO AJAM MADURA (Madurese Chicken Broth)

1 young tender chicken
½ lb. scalded bean sprouts
3 large new potatoes, boiled and sliced
lime or lemon juice to taste
¼ lb. peeled shrimp
½-inch-slice ginger
1½ teaspoons turmeric
8 small cloves garlic
2 small yellow onions
salt and pepper to taste

For garnish

4 cloves garlic, thickly sliced and fried in oil until brown
4 green onions with green leaves, chopped

Disjoint the chicken. Chop and pound fine the shrimp, ginger, turmeric, garlic and onions. Blend this mixture with the chicken pieces, thoroughly coating the chicken with it, and leave it aside for a few minutes. Now put the spiced chicken into a saucepan, cover with water, add salt to taste and simmer until tender.

When this is done, remove the chicken pieces, take the meat

off the bones and slice it fine. Arrange the meat on a deep plate with slices of boiled potato and bean sprouts. Pour the broth over it, sprinkle the sliced celery and fried garlic on top, squeeze over a little lime or lemon juice.

Sambal

Serve this soto accompanied by the following sambal: 5 Macadamia nuts fried in coconut oil, with fresh red chillies to taste, salt, and a $\frac{1}{2}$-inch by $\frac{1}{2}$-inch slice trasi which has been roasted or fried. Grind everything to a paste and moisten with a little soya sauce.

III. SOTO AJAM (Spicy Chicken Soup)

This soto has no accompanying sambal and is therefore not hot.

1 chicken (about 3 lbs.)
$\frac{1}{4}$-inch by $\frac{1}{4}$-inch slice trasi or blachan *or* $\frac{3}{8}$ teaspoon shrimp paste
4 green onions, sliced
3 Macadamia nuts or almonds, ground
1 curry leaf
2 tablespoons coconut oil
2 tablespoons chopped yellow onion
1 clove garlic, smashed and chopped
1 thin slice green ginger (about $\frac{1}{8}$-inch thick)
$\frac{3}{4}$ teaspoon turmeric
$\frac{3}{8}$ teaspoon coriander seeds, ground
salt to taste

Garnishes

$\frac{2}{3}$ cup cooked and drained Chinese vermicelli
$\frac{1}{2}$ cup chopped celery (the leafy end of the stalks)
$\frac{1}{2}$ cup chopped green onions (including the green part)
3 hard-boiled eggs, peeled and sliced
2 tablespoons fried onion flakes
3 new potatoes, boiled, peeled and sliced
$\frac{1}{2}$ lemon

55

Wash the chicken. Put it in a large saucepan, add about 7½–10 cups cold water, salt, the sliced green onions, and curry leaf. Bring to the boil and simmer until the chicken is tender. Remove the chicken, drain it and keep it aside. Heat the oil in a pan and fry the chopped yellow onion, ginger and garlic until light brown. Add these with the turmeric and coriander to the stock and simmer for a further 30 minutes.

Remove the skin and bones from the chicken and discard them. Cut the meat into thin strips. Put chicken strips and all the garnishing materials in a deep serving bowl. Pour the hot soup on top of these. Squeeze lemon juice over and serve.

IV. SOTO AJAM (Spicy Chicken Soup) (Vijsma's Version)

1 chicken
4 tablespoons chopped yellow onion
½-inch-piece green ginger, smashed and chopped
1¼ teaspoons laos powder
3 cloves garlic, smashed and chopped
1 stalk lemon grass, smashed and bruised but not sliced
1½ teaspoons ground coriander seeds
1½ teaspoons ground cumin seeds
1½ teaspoons ground black pepper
1½ teaspoons sugar
tamarind water made from a piece of tamarind pulp the size of a hazelnut (see p. 37)
salt to taste
lemon juice
light soya sauce
coconut oil

For garnish

⅔ cup cooked Chinese vermicelli
green onions, chopped
celery tops, chopped
fried onion flakes
unpeeled cucumber, diced

56

Disjoint the chicken. Cover it with water, add all the spices except the tamarind and simmer until the chicken is tender. Remove the pieces of chicken from the stock, take the meat from the bones and slice finely. Mix it with salt and tamarind water and stir-fry in a little hot coconut oil until brown.

Place the garnishing materials and the chicken meat in the bottom of a serving bowl. Pour the spiced stock over them. Squeeze in a little lemon juice, light soya sauce to taste, and serve.

SOTO BANDUNG (Garnished Tripe Broth)

2 cups thinly sliced tripe
5 cups beef bouillon
1 bunch Japanese radish (a white, long, mildly turnip-tasting
   vegetable)
a few green onion leaves, chopped
a few leafy stalks of celery, chopped
fried onion flakes
3 thin slices ginger, chopped
5 small cloves garlic
salt and pepper to taste
1 tablespoon coconut oil and more for deep frying
$\frac{1}{4}$ lb. dried white soya beans or lima beans which have been washed
   and soaked overnight
lemon or lime juice

Cover the tripe with water. Bring it to the boil, drain, and throw away the water, keeping the tripe aside. Peel, smash and chop the garlic. Heat 1 tablespoon coconut oil in a saucepan, and fry the garlic and ginger until it is light brown.

Pour in the beef bouillon, add the tripe, salt and pepper, and allow to simmer gently until the tripe is tender. When this is done add the chopped green onion leaves and the radish, which has been peeled and sliced into thin rounds. Continue cooking until the radish is tender but not too soft, then remove from the stove.

In the meantime, drain and dry the beans. Heat a lot of coconut oil and deep-fry the beans until they are crisp. Drain on paper toweling.

To serve, pour the soup into a deep bowl. Add the finely chopped celery, fried onion flakes and fried beans. Stir in a little of the sambal described below and squeeze a little lemon or lime juice to taste. Stir well. The bowl is now ready for the table.

Indonesians enjoy sprinkling this soto with crisply fried intestines and krupuk (see p. 116). We can replace these with crisp pork cracklings and potato chips.

Sambal

3 small red 'birdseye' chillies
3 Macadamia nuts or almonds
salt to taste

Finely chop and mince these together to form a paste.

SOTO DAGING (Garnished Beef Broth)

1½ lbs. shin beef or offal, or both
about ¼ lb. raw shrimp
2 yellow onions
12 cloves garlic
1-inch-piece green ginger
¾ teaspoon turmeric
salt to taste

For garnish
green onions
leafy ends of celery stalks
deep-fried garlic cloves, sliced
lime or lemon juice

Cover the meat with water, add salt and simmer until half cooked. Remove the meat, slice it into fine strips, then return the slices to the stock and allow to cool.

Peel and clean the shrimp. Chop and pound them until they

58

form a fine paste. Mix this with a little water, knead it thoroughly and strain out the juice through a fine sieve. Discard the shrimp pulp. When the meat stock is cool add the shrimp juice to it, return to the stove and reheat. Finely chop the onions, garlic, green ginger, turmeric and salt and add to the broth. Continue simmering gently until the meat is tender, then remove.

Pour the soup into a serving bowl, garnish with finely sliced onion leaves, celery, and fried garlic. Squeeze over it a little lime or lemon juice and stir in some of the sambal described below to taste.

Alternatively, serve the broth alone in a central bowl on the table, and place the garnishes, lemon juice and sambal on separate plates or bowls surrounding it. Each diner then places whatever vegetables he chooses on his own plate, pours broth over them, adds lime juice and sambal to individual taste and proceeds from there.

Sambal

6 fresh red chillies
10 Macadamia nuts or almonds
salt
beef stock

Mince chillies and nuts finely. Moisten them with a little beef stock, add salt to taste, and simmer on the stove until the juice has evaporated and the sambal is dry.

SAJUR BAJAM (Spinach Soup)

1½ heads of Chinese cabbage *or* ½ lb. young spinach
8-oz. package frozen corn *or* 1 small can whole kernels *or* the kernels stripped from 3 fresh cobs of corn
½ yellow onion, finely sliced
¾ teaspoon *or* ½-inch by ½-inch piece of trasi (blachan or shrimp paste)

2 cloves garlic, smashed and chopped
¾ teaspoon turmeric
¾ teaspoon laos powder (lengkuas) *or* 1 thin slice fresh laos
1 'birdseye' chilli, chopped
4 cups chicken stock
salt to taste

Fry the trasi until it smells cooked, cool it and pound it into a powder. Put the onion, garlic, trasi, turmeric, laos and chilli into the stock, bring to the boil and simmer for a few minutes. Add the corn and allow to cook. Add the roughly chopped spinach or Chinese cabbage and lightly cook. Adjust seasonings and serve.

SAJUR KARÉ (Curried Vegetable Soup)

½ lb. or more sliced or diced raw vegetables (cabbage, carrots,
   potatoes)
2 cups thin coconut milk (see p. 21)
¾ teaspoon turmeric
1 stalk lemon grass, finely sliced
2 curry leaves
⅜ teaspoon laos powder
1 clove garlic, smashed and chopped
1 yellow onion, finely chopped
melted coconut oil

In an electric blender mix the turmeric, laos, garlic, and onion into a smooth paste with a little melted coconut oil. Put this paste into a heated wok with extra oil if necessary and fry until it is cooked and aromatic. (You can tell that it is cooked when the contents no longer stick to the sides.)

Add the coconut milk, stir and bring to the boil. Add vegetables, curry leaves and lemon grass, and simmer uncovered until the vegetables are tender.

SAJUR AJAM (Tart Vegetable Soup)

About 1 lb. of any variety of vegetables (chopped green beans, corn
off the cob, shredded cabbage, raw peanuts, soaked kidney
beans, diced eggplant, zucchini rounds, etc.).
½–1 tablespoon raw beef, chicken or shrimp, chopped and lightly
stir-fried in a very little oil
2 fresh red chillies, sliced
½ yellow onion, chopped
1 curry leaf
2 cloves garlic, smashed and chopped (optional)
¼-inch by ¼-inch slice trasi or blachan *or* ¾ teaspoon shrimp paste
(fried)
tamarind water made from a piece of tamarind pulp the size of a
hazelnut (see p. 37) *or* 1 small tart cooking apple, peeled and
chopped
¾ teaspoon brown sugar (optional)

Make a stock by boiling the onion, chillies, curry leaf, sugar,
garlic and meat or shrimp and crumbled trasi in 4 cups water for
10 minutes. Add the vegetables in the order they require cooking.
Add the tamarind water when the vegetables are lightly cooked.
Stir, return to the boil and serve. If you use apple instead of
tamarind water, put it in to cook as you are adding the other
vegetables. Cook it to a pulp.

SAJUR BOBOR (Thick Vegetable Soup)

1 lb. very young spinach or any other green leafy vegetable,
roughly chopped
1 clove garlic, smashed and chopped
1 yellow onion, finely chopped
2 curry leaves
¾ teaspoon laos powder
3 Macadamia nuts
1½ teaspoons coriander seeds
brown sugar to taste (optional)
2 cups thin coconut milk
1 cup thick coconut milk

Pour the thin coconut milk into a saucepan, add the laos powder and the curry leaves and bring to the boil. In the meantime, grind the coriander seed and Macadamia nuts to a powder in an electric blender. Add sugar, onion and garlic to the machine and the necessary amount of water to keep the contents moving as the motor turns. Blend until you have a smooth paste.

Add this to the stock, stir and simmer a few minutes longer. Stir in the thick coconut milk and when it is hot, add the spinach. Allow it to cook lightly, stirring all the time. (This will only take a minute or two.) The soup is then ready.

SAJUR LODEH (Vegetable Soup)

1½ lbs. sliced or shredded vegetables (canned bamboo shoots, zucchini, eggplant, beans, cabbage, raw peanuts, etc.)
1 small peeled tomato, diced
2 teaspoons lean beef, chicken, or raw peeled shrimp, chopped
2 cups thin coconut milk
1 cup thick coconut milk
3 red chillies
1 yellow onion, finely chopped and its excess moisture squeezed out
½-inch by ½-inch slice trasi, or blachan *or* 1 teaspoon shrimp paste
2 cloves garlic
¾ teaspoon laos powder *or* 1 slice fresh laos (lengkuas)
¾ teaspoon brown sugar (optional)
coconut or peanut oil
salt

Finely chop the onion, chillies, garlic and trasi, then pound them to a fine paste in a mortar. Heat a little coconut or peanut oil (1 or 2 tablespoons) in a wok or deep pan and fry the meat and spice paste until they are cooked; then add the tomato and cook till soft. Add the thin coconut milk and laos, stir and bring to the boil. Add the vegetables in the order that they require cooking. When the vegetables are tender, stir in the thick coconut milk, add sugar and salt to taste, and serve.

SAJUR TERUNG ATAU LABU
(Eggplant or Zucchini Soup)

¾ teaspoon coriander seeds
a pinch of cumin seeds
1 large clove garlic, smashed and chopped
1½ yellow onions, chopped
⅜ teaspoon turmeric
3 Macadamia nuts or almonds
7 red chillies (fresh or dried) *or* 2 teaspoons ground chilli
2 cups coconut milk
2 small eggplants, zucchini, large cucumbers or squash, etc., sliced
  or diced
2 tablespoons chopped raw beef or chicken
2 curry leaves
1 thin slice green ginger, smashed and chopped
⅜ teaspoon laos powder (optional)
a squeeze of lemon or lime juice
2 tablespoons coconut or peanut oil
salt

Grind the coriander, cumin, nuts, turmeric and chilli (if you are using the dried variety) in a blender. Heat the oil in a saucepan and fry the onions and garlic until they are just yellow. Add the ground spices, ginger and sliced fresh chilli if you are using it and stir. Add the meat, salt to taste, cover with water and bring to the boil. Add laos powder and curry leaves and allow to simmer for about 15 minutes or until the meat is half cooked. Add coconut milk and simmer uncovered for about 10 minutes. Finally add the vegetables and continue cooking without a lid until it is tender but not overcooked. Remove from the stove, add lime or lemon juice, stir and serve.

Fish

PANGGANG IKAN BAWAL DJAWA
(Broiled Fish, Javanese Style)

1 small flatfish (flounder, fluke, dab, or gray sole)
5 fresh hot red chillies, finely sliced
2 tablespoons Javanese soya sauce (see p. 36) *or* 2 tablespoons dark
    soya sauce and 1 tablespoon brown sugar
2 teaspoons butter
1 thick slice lemon
1 clove garlic, peeled

Smash and chop the garlic and pour over it 1 tablespoon soya sauce. Dilute this with 1 tablespoon water. Clean and scale the fish and marinate it whole in this mixture for about 1 hour. Broil it over a *very low* charcoal fire, basting with the remaining marinade as it cooks. You can do this under the broiler, but the charcoal fire produces a more delicious result. When the fish is tender, remove from the fire and lay on a plate. Pour the melted butter over it, then sprinkle with a final spice mixture made from the sliced chillies, the rest of the soya sauce, and the lemon juice.

IKAN LAUT GORENG (Fried Fish)

1 whole sea fish (mullet, mackerel, red snapper, or other good
    frying fish)
salt
½ cup thick tamarind water (see p. 37), white vinegar, or lime or
    lemon juice
5 or 6 tablespoons peanut oil

Clean, scale and wash the fish. Make some slashes through the skin on each side. Mix the salt, tamarind water, vinegar or lemon juice with a little water and marinate the fish in this for at least 30 minutes, turning it about frequently.

Heat the oil in a pan or a wok. When it is hot, dry the fish with paper towels and fry first on one side, then on the other, until it is cooked. Turn it over only once, and then carefully, as the flesh may crumble.

PANGGANG BANDENG (Baked Mullet)

1 large mullet
6 fresh hot chillies (red)
2 cloves garlic
½–1 cup dark soya sauce
1 tablespoon brown sugar (optional)
juice of ½ lemon
butter or margarine
enough foil to wrap the fish

Clean, scale and wash the mullet, then make some slashes through the skin across each side. Chop the chillies and garlic coarsely, add the soya sauce, sugar and lemon juice. Marinate the fish in this sauce for at least 1 hour, turning it about occasionally. Grease one side of the foil with butter or margarine. Take the fish out of its marinade, place it on the greased foil, then spoon a little of the spiced marinade over it. Wrap it securely. Bake on top of a very low charcoal fire turning once or twice, or in a low oven on a cookie sheet. Allow about 20 minutes for the first pound and 10 minutes for each additional pound.

An alternative way of cooking would be not to use a foil wrapper for the fish but simply to lift it from its marinade, secure it in a wire broiling frame and bake on top of the barbecue, turning the whole frame to cook the other side.

ATJAR IKAN (Pickled Fish)

1 whole mullet about 8 inches long, cleaned and scaled
1½ teaspoons turmeric
salt

coconut or peanut oil for frying
4 fresh chillies, seeds removed, and cut into flower shapes (see p. 23)
3 teaspoons white vinegar
1 cup water
a few whole small white onions
4 Macadamia nuts

Rub the fish with turmeric and salt, slash it two or three times through the skin on each side, and fry until cooked in a wok or a pan, turning gently. If the fish is too big for the pan, you can cut it in two. Drain and set aside.

Grind the Macadamia nuts fine in an electric blender or crush them. Add the turmeric and mix. Heat a little oil in a pan and fry the turmeric and nut paste a little. Add the chillies, white onions, vinegar and water. Put the fish back in and simmer gently, stirring carefully, until the sauce is thicker and the fish is heated through.

SAMBAL GORENG UDANG (Chilli-fried Shrimp)

3 or 4 dried hot chillies *or* ¾–1½ teaspoons ground chilli *or* 1½ teaspoons sambal oelek
1 yellow onion, peeled, finely chopped, and its excess water squeezed out
2 cloves garlic, peeled, smashed and chopped
¾ teaspoon laos (lengkuas) powder *or* 1 slice fresh laos or green ginger
tamarind water made from a piece of tamarind the size of a hazelnut (see p. 37) *or* 1 tablespoon lemon juice
2 curry leaves
¾ lb. peeled raw shrimp
½ cup thick coconut milk
1 tablespoon coconut or peanut oil
salt to taste

Grind the chillies to a powder in a blender. Add onion, garlic, laos or ginger smashed and chopped, and oil, and blend in the machine until they are a fine paste. Heat a wok or frying pan on the stove (adding 1½ teaspoons oil if necessary). Add the ground paste and fry it until it is well brown and aromatic. Add the shrimp and stir until they are coated. Add the coconut milk, tamarind water or lemon juice and curry leaves and stir until everything is well mixed. Allow to bubble and continue stirring slowly until the gravy is dark and thick, the oil having 'come out,' that is, separated, from the rest of the gravy.

SATÉ BANDENG (Stuffed Fish Saté)

If you really want to impress a Javanese, just cook this dish successfully!

1 small mullet or bass, about 8 inches long
2 cups thick coconut milk, simmered until it has thickened a little,
    then allowed to cool
½ yellow onion, sliced
2 cloves garlic, smashed
2 tablespoons coconut oil
¾ teaspoon coriander seeds
a pinch of cumin seeds
¾ teaspoon trasi (blachan) or shrimp paste
1 small piece tamarind the size of a pea
½-inch-piece lemon grass, finely sliced
1½ teaspoons brown sugar

Wash and scale the fish, taking care not to perforate the skin. Massage it hard all over for some time in order to release the backbone from the flesh. If this is properly done, the time should come when the bone can be pulled out through a gill opening. Then press out *all* the meat and entrails through the gill hole, discarding the entrails but keeping aside all the flesh. Leave the fish skin whole but empty, pulling it inside out (through the gill opening) to remove all the flesh. Then wash out and turn right side in. Through all this, do *not* displace the head or tail or break the skin anywhere but at the gill hole. Remove all the bones from the flesh that you have kept aside and flake the flesh with your fingers.

Fry the sliced onion and garlic in 2 tablespoons heated coconut oil until they are well browned. Remove and keep aside. Fry the coriander, cumin and trasi whole and when cooked grind them and the onions to a fine paste in a blender, adding 5 tablespoons cooled thick coconut milk, the sugar and the tamarind as the blades turn. Throw in the flaked fish, lemon grass and brown sugar, and blend everything thoroughly.

Refill the fish skin with this mixture. Completely wrap the whole fish in greased foil and broil over a barbecue or in the oven. It will take about 20 minutes to cook.

A less artistic and dedicated cook could split the fish along one side and remove the bones and flesh. She could sew up the opening after stuffing the fish. This probably would not do in Indonesia, where the fish are grilled in more porous banana leaves; but with a sealed foil covering, no juices could escape anyway.

SATÉ UDANG (Shrimp Saté)

1 lb. raw jumbo shrimp, shelled and deveined
½ clove garlic, smashed and chopped
⅜ teaspoon *or* ¼-inch-slice trasi (blachan) or shrimp paste
1 stalk lemon grass *or* 1 tablespoon grated lemon peel
¾ teaspoon ground chilli
⅜ teaspoon salt
½ cup ground Macadamia nuts or fried peanuts
½ cup coconut milk
1 tablespoon lime or lemon juice
1 tablespoon peanut or coconut oil

Heat the oil in a pan. Fry the garlic and trasi for 1 minute. Add the rest of the ingredients and cook gently, stirring together until well blended. Do not allow to boil.

Thread the shrimp on skewers or saté sticks – about 4 shrimp per stick. Spread half the coating over them on one side and broil about 4 inches away from the heat under an electric broiler for 5 minutes. Turn them over, spread on the remaining paste and broil on the other side.

IKAN SEMUR DJAWA (Fish in Soya Sauce)

1 lb. fish steaks (cod, haddock, snapper salmon, grouper)
4 fresh red chillies, sliced
1 large yellow onion, chopped
3 cloves garlic, smashed and chopped
2 teaspoons laos powder (lengkuas)
2 tablespoons Javanese soya sauce *or* 2 tablespoons dark soya sauce
  plus 1 tablespoon brown sugar
2 tablespoons vinegar
3–4 tablespoons water
5 tablespoons tamarind water made from a walnut-sized piece of
  tamarind (see p. 37) *or* 5 tablespoons lemon juice
salt to taste
coconut or peanut oil

Soak the fish steaks in tamarind water or lemon juice for about 30 minutes. Dry them with paper towels. Heat about 6 tablespoons oil in a wok or a frying pan and fry the fish pieces until they are brown, turning them about carefully. Remove and set aside. Leaving only 2 tablespoons oil in the pan, fry the chillies, onions, garlic, and laos until soft. Add sugar if you are using it, then water, vinegar, soya sauce and salt to taste, and stir. Return the fish to the pan and allow to simmer gently until it is tender. This dish must not be allowed to cook dry. Remove the fish carefully to a serving plate and pour the gravy over it.

IKAN MASAK BALI (Fish Balinese Style)

2 small whole mullet or bass, cleaned and scaled
4 fresh red chillies, seeds removed

69

1½ teaspoons trasi (blachan) or ½-inch by ½-inch-slice hard trasi
1 small yellow onion
2 cloves garlic
1 slice green ginger
1½ teaspoons dark soya sauce
1 piece tamarind pulp, softened in a little warm water
a pinch of sugar (optional)
salt to taste
coconut or peanut oil
1 cup water

Rub the fish with tamarind and salt and shallow fry in heated oil until golden, turning carefully so as not to break the flesh. Set aside.

Put the chillies, onion, garlic and ginger through the fine blade of a grinder, then mash them to a pulp. Fry them in 1 tablespoon oil in a wok or wide pan until they are soft. Add water, soya sauce and sugar (if you are using it). Return the fish to the pan and let the broth simmer gently without a lid until the dish is almost dry, when it is ready to serve.

GULÉ IKAN PADANG (Padang Fish Curry) (Sumatra)

1 large whole fish *or* 4 very small fish, cleaned and scaled, dried with paper towels, and rubbed with tamarind pulp and salt
1½ large yellow onions, finely chopped
2 teaspoons laos powder
1½ teaspoons turmeric
4 hot dried chillies
1 tablespoon coconut or vegetable oil
1 stalk lemon grass, sliced
1½ cups thick coconut milk
juice of ½ lemon
salt to taste

Mash all the spices except the lemon grass (with the onions) in a mortar or with a little oil in an electric blender. Heat the coconut or vegetable oil in a wok and fry this paste until light brown. Add the coconut milk and lemon grass and bring to the boil. Put in the fish and simmer gently, uncovered, turning the fish about until it is cooked and adding salt to taste. Finally add the lemon juice, stir it in, and serve. (Chicken, fish, lamb or tripe can be used for this curry.)

GULÉ UDANG DENGAN LABU KUNING
(Shrimp and Winter Squash or Zucchini Curry) (Sumatra)

1 lb. peeled shrimp (preferably raw)
⅓ medium-sized zucchini or winter squash, peeled, cored and diced
4 fresh red chillies
1 large yellow onion
1 teaspoon turmeric
⅜ teaspoon laos powder
1 stalk lemon grass, smashed and bruised but not sliced
1 cup thick coconut milk
a few basil leaves *or* 2 curry leaves
a squeeze of lemon juice
salt to taste

Put the chillies and onion through the fine blade of a grinder. Mix them with the turmeric and laos, add 1 cup cold water and cook this mixture into a broth adding the basil, lemon grass, and a squeeze of lemon juice. When it comes to the boil, add the shrimp and the zucchini and simmer gently until they are half cooked. Add the thick coconut milk, salt to taste, and cook, uncovered, until the shrimp and vegetable are ready.

PANGÉ IKAN (Fish Stew) (Sumatra)

1 whole fish (mackerel, bonito, tuna, etc.)
1 tablespoon ground chilli
1 large yellow onion
3 cloves garlic
3 Macadamia nuts

4 whole thin slices lemon with skin
a few basil leaves, roughly chopped
salt to taste

Chop the onion, garlic, nuts and pound them with the chilli to a paste. Put this into a wok or a shallow pan *without* any oil, together with the fish, the lemon slices and the basil leaves. Mix together gently until the fish is coated and everything is evenly distributed. Take care not to break the fish. Pour in enough water barely to cover the fish, and simmer over a low fire without a lid until the fish is cooked. Do not stir this dish with a spoon as it cooks. It is enough to shake the pan occasionally. Adjust the salt before serving.

GULÉ MASIN IKAN (Tasty Fish Curry) (Sumatra)

1 lb. fish (mackerel, bonito, Spanish mackerel, or any curry
    fish)
2 cups thick coconut milk
2 yellow onions
4 cloves garlic, smashed and chopped
4 Macadamia nuts, crushed
½-inch-slice ginger, smashed and chopped
¾ teaspoon turmeric
2 fresh hot chillies
2 lemon slices with skin
a few basil leaves, roughly chopped
salt to taste
5 tablespoons tamarind water made from a walnut-sized piece of
    tamarind (see p. 37)

Scale, wash and slice the fish into steaks. Slice the onions finely lengthwise. Cut the chillies in half lengthwise. Mash the garlic, turmeric, nuts and ginger to a fine paste. Put this into a shallow pan or wok, then add the coconut milk and bring to the boil. Then add the onions, chillies, and basil. Let the gravy simmer, uncovered, for a while until it reduces considerably and thickens. Then put in the fish and after that the lemon slices. Allow to

72

bubble, still uncovered, stirring gently all the while as it will curdle otherwise. Add the tamarind water and salt to taste when the fish is cooked.

IKAN TJUKA (Fish in Vinegar) (Sumatra)

1 lb. fish (mackerel, mullet, bonito, Spanish mackerel,
    whiting, etc.)
1 yellow onion
2 cloves garlic
1-inch-piece green ginger, smashed and chopped
1 cup water
salt
1 tablespoon vinegar (or more)
2 fresh red chillies
coconut or peanut oil

Clean, scale and cut the fish into steaks, or leave it whole. Rub it with salt and fry gently until cooked in sufficient coconut oil or peanut oil in a wok. Remove and keep aside. Slice the onion coarsely, cut each garlic clove into four pieces, and slice the chillies in two down the middle. Leaving only 1 tablespoon oil in the pan, fry the onions, garlic, chillies and ginger until they are soft. Add about 1 cup water, put in the fish, add vinegar and salt. Bring to the boil, allow to blend for a few minutes, and serve.

Poultry

AJAM GORENG DJAWA (Fried Chicken) (Java)

1 small, tender chicken
2 fresh chillies, seeds removed
1 yellow onion, chopped
1½ teaspoons coriander seeds
2 Macadamia nuts or almonds
¾ teaspoon turmeric
¾ teaspoon laos powder
1 stalk lemon grass, finely sliced
salt to taste
sugar to taste (optional)
coconut or peanut oil for frying
1 cup coconut milk

Cut the chicken into serving pieces. Grind the coriander seeds to a powder in an electric blender. Add the nuts and grind them. Add the chillies, onion, turmeric and laos to the machine and grind them to a paste. Add the coconut milk to keep the blades working effectively, and blend everything together well in the machine. Pour the mixture into a wok, add the lemon grass, salt and sugar to taste. Then put in the chicken pieces, stir well, and let them marinate for an hour or so if you have time. Put the pan on the heat and bring to the boil. Allow to simmer gently until the chicken is tender and the gravy has evaporated. Remove from the stove and lift out the chicken pieces. Finally, heat plenty of oil in a pan and fry the spiced chicken pieces until they are brown.

AJAM BUMBU RUDJAK
(Chicken Cooked in 'Rudjak' Spices)

1 tender chicken
3 Macadamia nuts
2 cloves garlic

1½ yellow onions
6 fresh chillies *or* 3 teaspoons sambal oelek
1½ teaspoons coriander seeds
⅜ teaspoon turmeric
¾ teaspoon laos powder *or* 1 slice laos (lengkuas)
2 curry leaves
1½ cups thick coconut milk
¾ teaspoon trasi (blachan) or shrimp paste (optional)
1 stalk lemon grass
a dash of dark soya sauce
brown sugar to taste
salt to taste
1 tablespoon coconut oil

Cut the chicken into curry pieces (see p. 24). Grind the coriander seeds to a powder in a blender. Add the Macadamia nuts, turmeric and laos, and blend. Chop the garlic, onions and chillies and mash them together with the ground spices and the trasi to a fine paste. Heat the oil in a wok and fry the spices until they are cooked. Add the coconut milk, the lemon grass bruised but not sliced, the curry leaves, chicken pieces, sugar, salt and the dark soya sauce, and stir. Bring to the boil and cook, uncovered, until the chicken is tender and the gravy thick.

AJAM PANGGANG BUMBU RUDJAK
(Broiled Chicken with 'Rudjak' Spices)

1 young chicken
1 yellow onion
2 cloves garlic
3 chillies
¾ teaspoon trasi (blachan) or shrimp paste, roasted in foil (see p. 28)
1½ teaspoons laos powder (lengkuas) *or* 2 slices fresh laos
1 stalk lemon grass *or* ½ teaspoon grated orange peel
1 cup thick coconut milk
1 tablespoon lemon juice *or* tamarind water made from a piece of tamarind the size of a hazelnut (see p. 37)
1½ teaspoons brown sugar
salt to taste

Cut the chicken down the breastbone and open it out in one flat piece with the legs skewered down to the back so that the bird remains flat during first cooking.

Put the chillies, onions, garlic, trasi and laos through a mincer, then mash them in a mortar to a fine paste. Coat the chicken all over with this paste and let it stand for a while for the spices to penetrate.

Put the coconut milk, lemon grass, sugar, salt and lemon juice or tamarind water in a shallow pan big enough to hold the chicken. Put in the chicken and spices and bring to the boil. Simmer gently without a lid, spooning sauce and spices over the bird all the time until the chicken is tender and the sauce has dried out.

Remove the chicken and roast it flat over a very low charcoal fire or barbecue until brown, spooning over the remaining oily spices from the pan as it cooks. This final roasting in all the 'panggang' recipes can be done on a rack over a baking dish in the oven, basting with left-over spices and oil, but it will not be as good as the barbecued version.

AJAM SEMUR DJAWA (Chicken in Soya Sauce) (Java)

1 chicken
2 fresh red chillies
1 yellow onion
2 cloves garlic
1½ teaspoons laos powder (lengkuas) *or* 2 slices fresh laos (optional)
2 cups water
1 tablespoon dark soya sauce
1½ teaspoons brown sugar
salt
2 teaspoons white vinegar
1 tomato, peeled and chopped (optional)
coconut or peanut oil

Clean and cut the chicken into frying pieces with bone (see p. 24). Rub them with vinegar and salt and deep-fry in coconut or peanut oil until brown. Remove and drain.

Put the chillies, onions, garlic and laos through the fine blade of a grinder, then pound in a mortar until you have a fine paste. Fry this in 1 tablespoon oil until it smells cooked. Add 2 cups water with the vinegar, soya sauce, sugar and tomato, and cook the chicken in this sauce until it is tender. Do not let semur become dry.

PETJEL AJAM (Chicken in Coconut Milk)

¾ lb. cooked chicken (or broil some uncooked chicken breasts with
  salt)
2 cups thick coconut milk
1 yellow onion, finely chopped
1 clove garlic, smashed and chopped
1-inch-piece green ginger, smashed and chopped
¾ teaspoon ground chilli
basil leaves
1 tablespoon coriander seeds
2 tablespoons coconut oil

Grind the coriander seeds to a powder. Heat the oil in a wok and fry the garlic and onion. Add the other spices, coconut milk and basil leaves. Dice the chicken meat and put it into the sauce. Cook slowly, without a lid, stirring all the while for 15 minutes.

SATÉ AJAM (Chicken Saté)

3 whole chicken breasts

Marinade

2 cloves garlic, smashed and chopped
2 tablespoons dark soya sauce
2 tablespoons water

Peanut sauce

1 tablespoon coconut or peanut oil
1 small yellow onion, chopped

1½ teaspoons ground chilli
5 Macadamia nuts
1½ teaspoons brown sugar (optional)
4 oz. raw peanuts, freshly fried until cooked in a smear of oil in a
  pan on top of the stove *or* 4 oz. crunchy peanut butter
¾ cup thin coconut milk or water
1 tablespoon lime or lemon juice
1½ tablespoons Javanese soya sauce (see p. 36) *or* 1 tablespoon dark
  soya sauce with 1 tablespoon brown sugar melted in it
salt to taste

Skin and bone the chicken breasts. Cut the meat into ½-inch cubes, prick all over with a fork, and thread the cubes on to skewers or saté sticks, leaving about 3 inches at the holding end of the skewer. Combine the marinade ingredients in a flat dish and soak the skewers of meat in this for about 30 minutes.

In an electric blender or on a good grinding stone, grind the onion, Macadamia nuts, chilli, sugar and peanuts or peanut butter until they form a fine paste, adding the oil if necessary to keep the blades turning. Heat the oil in a wok (if you haven't already mixed it into the spice paste) and fry the spice paste a little. Add the coconut milk or water and cook until the sauce is thick but not heavy. Keep the sauce warm.

In the meantime broil the skewers of meat over a low charcoal barbecue fire or, less desirably, under an electric broiler until they are cooked. Just before serving, stir the lemon juice and Javanese soya sauce into the peanut mixture on the stove, adding salt to taste.

Arrange the skewers on a serving plate, pour the peanut sauce over the top, and serve with or without rice. If you prefer it hotter, scatter some minced fresh red chilli on top of the sauce.

AJAM BALI (Balinese Chicken)

1 small chicken
butter or peanut oil
1 clove garlic
1 medium yellow onion

78

1 tablespoon coriander, ground
5 Macadamia nuts
¼-inch-piece green ginger
2 teaspoons dark soya sauce
1½ teaspoons brown sugar
a dash of white vinegar
1 cup water

Cut the chicken down the breastbone, flatten it out and fry it in butter or peanut oil until brown and cooked. Lift out and keep aside.

Put the garlic, onion, nuts, ginger and chillies through the fine blade of a grinder, then mash them into a paste. Heat a little oil in a wok and fry the spices until they smell cooked. Add the water, soya sauce, sugar and vinegar, and stir. Put in the chicken and spoon the sauce over it, warming everything through, and serve.

AJAM GORENG PADANG (Fried Chicken) (Sumatra)

1 chicken
1 large clove garlic
1½ yellow onions
2 fresh chillies, seeds removed, *or* 1½ teaspoons sambal oelek
⅜ teaspoon turmeric
1 stalk lemon grass, bruised but not sliced
3 cups coconut milk (thin)
vegetable oil for frying

Finely chop the garlic, onions and chillies and then mash them into a fine paste with the turmeric. Cut the chicken into serving pieces and rub them well with the spice paste. Leave to stand for a little while. Put the chicken and spices into a pan, pour the coconut milk over them, add the lemon grass, and allow to simmer without a lid for about 30 minutes, spooning the sauce over the chicken pieces as they cook. Remove from the stove, lift chicken from the pan, and fry until brown or broil, basting with oil.

SINGGANG AJAM (Broiled Chicken) (Sumatra)

1 young chicken
⅜ teaspoon turmeric
1 stalk lemon grass, finely sliced
1 or 2 orange or other citrus leaves (optional) *or* basil
3 or 4 teaspoons ground chilli, according to taste
1 yellow onion, finely chopped
3 cloves garlic, smashed and chopped
½-inch-slice green ginger, smashed and chopped
10 black peppercorns, ground
salt to taste
2 cups thick coconut milk

Cut the chicken down the breastbone and truss flat, 'panggang' style (see p. 24). Mash the onions, garlic, ginger, peppercorns, chilli and turmeric in a mortar to a fine paste. Spread this paste over the chicken and leave it to stand for 1 hour while the spices penetrate. Put the coconut milk, lemon grass and citrus or basil leaves into a shallow pan large enough to hold the chicken. Lower in the flattened chicken, cover and simmer gently until the chicken is tender and the broth has become thick and oily. Lift out the chicken and broil over a very low charcoal fire until brown. Moisten it occasionally with juices from the pan.

OPOR AJAM (Chicken White Curry)

1 chicken
3 Macadamia nuts
1 tablespoon coriander seeds
⅜ teaspoon cumin seeds
⅜ teaspoon fennel seeds (optional)
12 peppercorns
1 large yellow onion
2 cloves garlic
½-inch-slice green ginger
¼-inch-piece cinnamon bark

80

a pinch of laos powder (optional)
3 cloves
coconut or peanut oil
1 stalk lemon grass
2 curry leaves
2 cups thick coconut milk
salt
juice of $\frac{1}{2}$ lemon, or to taste

Cut the chicken into curry pieces (see p. 24). Cut the onion into fine slices. Grind all the dry spices into a powder in an electric blender (coriander, cumin, fennel, peppercorns, cloves and cinnamon), add the garlic, Macadamia nuts and ginger, and grind to a paste, adding a little coconut or peanut oil to keep the blades turning.

Heat 1 tablespoon oil in a wok or a pan and fry the sliced onions until soft. Add the spice paste and the chicken pieces and stir together, turning everything about until the chicken is well coated. Add a dash of water, the curry leaves, laos and lemon grass, and partially cook the chicken. Then add the coconut milk, cover and simmer gently until the chicken is cooked and tender. Finally add the lemon juice and salt to taste, stir and serve.

GULÉ AJAM (Chicken Curry)

1 chicken
1-inch-piece green ginger
3 cloves
10 black peppercorns
$\frac{3}{8}$ teaspoon cumin seeds
$\frac{3}{8}$ teaspoon fennel seeds
1$\frac{1}{2}$ teaspoons coriander seeds
$\frac{3}{8}$ teaspoon turmeric
$\frac{1}{2}$-inch-piece cinnamon bark
7 dried chillies
1 large yellow onion, chopped

81

2 cloves garlic
3 Macadamia nuts or almonds
1-inch-stem lemon grass, bruised
1 large tomato
1 tablespoon lemon or lime juice
2 oz. grated coconut flesh or dried grated coconut
2 cups thick coconut milk
salt to taste
1 tablespoon coconut or peanut oil

Cut the chicken into curry pieces (see p. 24). Heat the oil in a pan and fry the onion until soft with the whole cloves and cinnamon bark. In an electric blender, grind the rest of the dry spices to a powder. Add the nuts and grind, then the garlic and grind. Finally add the tomato to the machine and a little water if necessary, and blend everything well until you have a smooth paste. Add this to the onions in the pan together with a little more water; then add the lemon grass.

In a separate pan, fry the grated coconut flesh without oil until it is yellow, remove, and grind it finely. Add this to the spice broth.

Salt the pieces of chicken, put them in the broth and simmer for about 15 minutes until the chicken is half cooked. Add the coconut milk and continue cooking until the chicken is tender. Add the lime or lemon juice 5 minutes before the cooking is completed. Stir, adjust the seasoning, and serve.

KALIO AJAM (Wet Chicken Curry) (Sumatra)

1 chicken
1 tablespoon ground chilli, or to taste
3 Macadamia nuts
3–4 cups thin coconut milk
1 yellow onion
3 cloves garlic
1-inch-piece green ginger
$\frac{3}{4}$ teaspoon turmeric

1 stem lemon grass, sliced
citrus leaf (optional)
a squeeze of lemon or lime juice
salt

Cut the chicken into curry pieces (see p. 24). Finely chop the nuts,
onion, garlic and ginger, and mash them into a fine paste with the
turmeric and ground chilli. Stir this into the coconut milk in a
wide pan. Add the lemon grass and citrus leaf, put it on the stove
and bring to the boil. Put in the chicken pieces and boil vigorously
without a lid until the chicken is half cooked. Then turn down the
stove and simmer gently, still uncovered, until the chicken is
tender and the broth has reduced but is still plentiful. Take the
saucepan off the stove, add a squeeze of lemon juice and salt to
taste, and serve.

AJAM KUNING (Yellow Chicken)

This recipe contains no chillies and so would be a 'safe' dish for
uncertain guests.

1 chicken, cut into curry pieces (see p. 24)
10 Macadamia nuts
½-inch-piece green ginger, smashed and chopped
¾ teaspoon peppercorns
1½ teaspoons coriander seeds
¾ teaspoon cumin seeds
1½ teaspoons ground turmeric
1 yellow onion, finely chopped
2 cloves garlic, smashed and chopped
1½ teaspoons salt
2 points star anise
3 cloves
2 curry leaves
1½ cups thin coconut milk
½ cup thick coconut milk

In an electric blender, grind the peppercorns, coriander, cumin
and turmeric to a powder. Add the nuts, ginger, garlic and onion

and grind to a paste, adding oil if necessary to keep the blades turning.

Fry the paste gently in a wok until it is cooked. Add the chicken pieces and stir until the meat is well coated. Add the whole star anise, cloves and curry leaves. Now add the thin coconut milk and salt to taste, and simmer gently with a lid on until the chicken is tender. Remove the lid, add the thick coconut milk, and cook, uncovered, until the gravy is almost dry.

Meat

RATAMI'S SATÉ

1 lb. broiling steak (rump) or boned leg of lamb
¾ teaspoon salt
2 cloves garlic, smashed and chopped
½ yellow onion, grated
1 tablespoon brown sugar
4½ teaspoons lemon juice
1½ teaspoons tamarind juice made from a peanut-sized piece
    tamarind (see p. 37) (optional)
2 tablespoons dark soya sauce

Combine all the ingredients except the meat to make a marinade. Cut the meat into ½-inch cubes and soak them in the marinade for at least 30 minutes. Then thread the cubes on skewers or saté sticks, leaving 3 inches at the holding end, and broil them, basting with what is left of the marinade. The broiling is best done over a charcoal fire or a low barbecue fire, though an electric broiler or even a griddle on top of the stove is acceptable.

Place the satés (skewers and all) on a large heated plate and spoon peanut sauce, described below, over them. Garnish with fried onion flakes and finish with a squeeze of lime or lemon juice. Guests help themselves.

Ratami's peanut sauce

4 oz. raw peanuts, freshly roasted in a smear of oil in a pan on top
    of the stove, then roughly ground, *or* 4 oz. crunchy peanut butter
1 yellow onion, grated or minced
1 cup thick coconut milk
1 tablespoon brown sugar
1½ teaspoons ground hot chilli
1 stem lemon grass, sliced fine, *or* 1-inch-piece finely pared lemon peel
½ curry leaf
salt and pepper to taste

Combine all the ingredients, and bring to the boil, adding water if the sauce is too thick.

(In sauces for Indonesian food, you can always use crunchy peanut butter instead of roasting and grinding your own peanuts. However, the dish will suffer a little as a result, and the extra trouble of preparing raw peanuts is worth it.)

SATÉ BUMBU (Spiced Saté)

1 lb. steak (top round or round steak is best for this recipe)
1 tablespoon coconut oil or ghee
1 small yellow onion, chopped
2 cloves garlic
2 dried 'birdseye' chillies
2 Macadamia nuts
1½ teaspoons coriander seeds
¾ teaspoon turmeric
½-inch-slice green ginger
¼ teaspoon laos powder
1 tablespoon brown sugar
1 curry leaf
1 lemon or orange leaf (optional)
¾ cup thick coconut milk

Cut the meat into 1-inch cubes. Grind the coriander, chillies, nuts and turmeric to a powder in an electric blender. Add the ginger, garlic and onions, and blend to a smooth paste, adding coconut oil or melted ghee to keep the blades turning. Heat a wok or shallow pan, add the spice paste and fry until it no longer sticks to the pan. Add the laos, brown sugar, curry leaf, lemon leaf and coconut milk; stir and bring to the boil. Add the meat and cook, uncovered, until the sauce is dry.

Lift out the cubes of meat, thread them on skewers or saté sticks, leaving 3 inches at the holding end, and roast over a low charcoal fire or under the broiler, basting with what is left of the spices in the pan. Do not add any other sauce.

You can also make this saté with lamb cubes or calf's liver.

SATÉ KAMBING BUMBU KETJAP
(Lamb and Soya Saté)

1 leg of lamb, boned (about 2½ lbs.)

For the marinade

2 cloves garlic, smashed and chopped
2 tablespoons dark soya sauce
¾ teaspoon salt
⅜ teaspoon pepper

Cut the meat into ½-inch cubes and thread them on skewers or saté sticks, leaving 3 inches at the holding end. Prick all over with a fork. Combine all the marinade ingredients and pour over the meat. Allow it to marinate in a flat dish for 1 hour. Broil over a low charcoal fire or under the broiler. Place the skewers on a large plate, pour over them the sauce described below and serve.

Sauce

¼ cup finely chopped onions
4 Macadamia nuts, ground (optional)
fresh hot chilli to taste, sliced
2 tablespoons lime or lemon juice
¾ cup Javanese soya sauce (see p. 36) *or* ¾ cup soya sauce and
    ⅜ cup brown sugar
salt and pepper

Combine all the ingredients with a little water and stew until the spices are soft.

MAGBUB (Ground Lamb Saté) (West Java)

1 lb. boned raw leg of lamb, ground with its fat
¼ cup sliced yellow onion
4 small cloves garlic, sliced
2 teaspoons coriander seeds
tamarind juice made from a walnut-sized piece of tamarind pulp
    (see p. 37)

¼ cup brown sugar
¼ cup thick coconut milk, boiled
sheep's caul cut into 2-inch by 1-inch strips – for non-Moslems
  streaky bacon would do very well
¼ cup coconut or peanut oil
salt to taste

Heat the oil in a pan and fry the onion and garlic slices until they are well browned and crisp. Remove from the pan and keep aside. Fry the coriander seeds until cooked (a short time), add the tamarind juice and simmer briefly. In an electric blender, grind the coriander to a powder. Add the tamarind, salt, onions, garlic, brown sugar and coconut milk, and blend. Combine this mixture with the minced lamb and mix well. Allow to stand for a while.

Take a rounded teaspoon of the mixture, place on a piece of bacon or sheep's caul and roll up like a sausage roll. Thread 3 of these rolls crosswise on a skewer or saté stick, leaving 3 inches at the holding end. Continue in this way until all the ingredients are used up. Wrap each skewered bundle securely in foil and broil over a barbecue or under the broiler. Unwrap and serve on the skewers.

SATÉ PADANG (Sumatra)

1 lb. heart, liver or tripe
1 tablespoon coriander seeds
¾ teaspoon cumin seeds
5 peppercorns
10 dried chillies
½ yellow onion, chopped
2 cloves garlic
¾ teaspoon laos powder
½-inch-slice green ginger
⅜ teaspoon turmeric
1 stem lemon grass, sliced
2 citrus (lemon or orange) leaves
salt to taste
3 tablespoons rice flour or cornstarch

In an electric blender, grind all the dry seeds and chillies to a powder. Add the laos, turmeric, onions, garlic and ginger, and grind to a paste, adding a little water to help the blades turn.

Cut the meat into cubes. Mix it with half the spice paste in a saucepan, add half the lemon grass, 1 lemon leaf and salt to taste. Add water to cover and simmer until the meat is three-quarters cooked. Lift out the cubes of meat, thread on to skewers, leaving 3 inches at the holding end, and broil over a low charcoal fire or under the broiler, sprinkling occasionally with the broth.

Add the rest of the spices and leaves to the broth and continue simmering without a lid until they are cooked. Then mix the cornstarch or rice flour to a paste with a little water, add it to the broth and cook until it thickens. Pour over the saté and serve.

ABON DAGING (Shredded Meat)

1 lb. top round in one piece
1½ teaspoons ground coriander
¾ teaspoon laos powder (lengkuas)
1½ teaspoons brown sugar
½ cup thick coconut milk
1 clove garlic, smashed and chopped (optional)
a little coconut or peanut oil
a few dried chillies (to taste), broken up
fried onion flakes from 1 yellow onion (see p. 22)

Just cover the meat with water and simmer gently for some hours until it is tender and ready to fall apart. Remove from the water, allow to drain and dry. Pound the meat with a meat hammer to soften it, then shred it very, very finely until it is a light nest of fibres. Finely mash the garlic, sugar, laos and coriander and mix with the coconut milk. Add this to the shredded meat in a bowl and knead everything together until well mixed. Spread the mixture on a tray in a low oven and let it dry out.

Heat some oil in a frying pan, put in the meat and fry until it is dry. Remove the meat from the pan and squeeze out all the oil through a sieve. Allow to cool, tease the shreds once more and mix with dried chillies to taste and fried onion flakes.

Abon can be stored in a screwtop jar up to a month and used in small quantities to flavour rice.

SAMBAL GORENG HATI (Chilli-fried Liver)

1 lb. diced liver (any kind)
4 teaspoons ground chilli *or* 12 dried hot chillies *or* 2 tablespoons sambal oelek
1½ yellow onions
3 cloves garlic
¾ teaspoon trasi *or* ½-inch-cube hard trasi (blachan)
1½ teaspoons laos powder (lengkuas) *or* 2 slices fresh laos
1½-inch-stem lemon grass (sliced) (optional)
3 curry leaves
1½ teaspoons brown sugar
1 cup thick coconut milk
½ ripe tomato, peeled and mashed, *or* a squeeze of lemon juice
coconut oil

Put the onions, garlic, chilli and trasi through the fine blade of a grinder and then mash them to a fine paste. Heat about 2 tablespoons coconut oil in a wok or a shallow frying pan and fry the spices until they are well browned and aromatic. Add the liver and fry until it changes colour. Add laos, curry leaves, lemon grass, tomato (or lemon juice), sugar and coconut milk. Stir and cook, uncovered, until the sauce thickens and reduces and its oil 'comes out.'

This dish can be made using half the amount of liver and the same weight of green beans.

KARÉ DJAWA (Javanese Curry)

1 lb. stewing steak *or* ½ lb. stewing steak and ½ lb. new potatoes, diced
¼ small cabbage, roughly sliced (optional)

1 tablespoon coriander seeds
¾ teaspoon cumin seeds
1½ teaspoons ground chilli
¾ teaspoon turmeric
½-inch-slice hard trasi (blachan) *or* ½ teaspoon trasi
3 cloves garlic, smashed and chopped
1 yellow onion, chopped
½-inch-slice green ginger, smashed and chopped
3 Macadamia nuts
¾ teaspoon laos powder (lengkuas) *or* 1 slice fresh laos
3 curry leaves
1 stem lemon grass, sliced fine, *or* 2 citrus leaves *or* 1 slice thinly
    pared lemon peel
½ cup thick coconut milk
salt to taste
a dash of vinegar *or* a squeeze of lemon juice
coconut or peanut oil

Grind the coriander, cumin, chilli and turmeric to a powder in an electric blender. Add the trasi, nuts, ginger, garlic and onion one by one in that order, and grind to a fine paste, adding oil if necessary to keep the blades turning.

Heat a wok or a pan on the stove and fry the spice paste until it no longer adheres to the pan. Dice the beef and add it to the paste. Cover with water, add the laos, curry leaves, lemon grass and salt. Put on a lid and simmer until the meat is about three-quarters done. Now add the potatoes, if you are using them, and when they are nearly cooked the cabbage, if used, and the thick coconut milk. Stir, allow the cabbage to wilt, then add the lemon juice or vinegar, and serve.

RENDANG (Sumatra)

Rendang is native to Padang, and cooked to West Sumatran taste is *very* hot. The amounts given here are average Indonesian measures for this dish, but you can adjust them to suit your own taste by using less of the potent ingredients, such as the chillies.

1 lb. steak (rump, top round, chuck)
2 tablespoons hot chillies *or* 6 teaspoons ground chilli
1½-inch-slice green ginger, smashed and chopped
1 or 2 cloves garlic, smashed and chopped
1 medium yellow onion, chopped
¾ teaspoon coriander seeds (optional)
⅜ teaspoon turmeric
2 lemon leaves *or* 2 curry leaves
1 stalk lemon grass, bruised but not sliced
2 cups thick coconut milk
salt to taste

In an electric blender, grind the coriander, chillies, turmeric, ginger, garlic and onion in that order, adding a little coconut milk to allow the blades to turn. Thoroughly blend spice paste and coconut milk. Pour this mixture into a wok or a frying pan. Cut the meat into 2-inch squares and stir into the coconut milk broth with the lemon leaves, lemon grass and salt to taste. Bring to the boil and cook without a lid over a high heat until the gravy is almost dry. Turn the heat down low and cook until the oil comes out of what is left of the gravy. Then, taking care to stir constantly, let the meat and its spices fry in the resulting oil until the dish is really dry and the meat has turned dark brown but is not burnt. This last process is the crucial one for rendang: the whole quality of the dish depends on the care with which it is done.

LAPIS DAGING SEMARANG
(Beef Slices, Semarang Style)

1 lb. rump steak (top round or round will do, but takes a little more cooking)
1 large yellow onion
3 cloves garlic
10 peppercorns
a pinch of nutmeg (optional)
¼ cup dark soya sauce
¼ cup brown sugar (optional)

1 more yellow onion, thinly sliced lengthwise
1 large ripe tomato, peeled and chopped
1 tablespoon butter or coconut oil

Slice the meat into small escalopes and beat them out thinly.
Grind the peppercorns. Finely chop the large onion and the
garlic and then mash them to a fine paste. Combine this with
the pepper, nutmeg, sugar and soya sauce. Marinate the meat
slices in this sauce for 30 minutes to 1 hour.

Heat the oil in a wok or a pan, add the sliced onion and fry it
until soft. Add the meat slices and marinade, and stir-fry for 1
minute. Then add the tomato and a little water. Stir and allow to
cook uncovered until the meat is tender, the tomato soft and
there is not too much gravy.

To cook this dish to Sumatran taste, do not add sugar at any
stage, but add a stick of cinnamon and two whole cloves during
the final cooking.

DAGING MASAK BALI (Meat Balinese Style)

1 lb. round steak or pork chop meat, thinly sliced
6–8 fresh red chillies without seeds
1½ teaspoons trasi (blachan) *or* 1-inch-slice hard trasi
1 yellow onion
4 cloves garlic
1 tablespoon brown sugar
1-inch-slice green ginger
2 tablespoons dark soya sauce
1 tablespoon lemon juice
salt to taste
1 cup water
coconut or peanut oil

Put the chillies, trasi, onion, garlic and green ginger through the
fine blade of a grinder, then mash them into a paste in a mortar.
Heat a little oil in a wok and fry the spices until soft. Add the
meat slices and stir-fry until they change colour. Add the water,
sugar, soya sauce, lemon juice and salt, and simmer, uncovered,

until the meat is tender and the gravy dry. Add more water if the dish threatens to become dry before the meat is cooked.

SEMUR DAGING (Beef in Soya Sauce)

2 lbs. stewing steak, cut into cubes
1 yellow onion, finely chopped
3 cloves garlic, smashed and chopped
½-inch-slice green ginger (optional), smashed and chopped
¾ teaspoon nutmeg
a dash of black pepper
2 whole cloves
1 tablespoon brown sugar
2 tablespoons dark soya sauce
salt to taste
1 tablespoon lemon juice (optional)
coconut or peanut oil

Fry the onion, garlic, ginger, nutmeg, pepper and cloves in oil until the onions are soft. Add the meat and fry until it changes colour. Add the sugar, soya sauce, lemon juice and salt to taste. Add enough water to cover, put on the lid and simmer until the meat is tender.

If you substituted ½–1 tablespoon ground chilli for the soya sauce you would have *Daging Madura*.

GULÉ

Gulé is a curry of Indian or Arab origin. It is found in various forms in all parts of Indonesia. Especially interesting is the way the basic dish is adapted to conform to the general food habits of the region in which it is cooked. To illustrate this, and perhaps to reflect a little on the regional practices themselves, I am including three versions of gulé here. The recipe from Central Java contains sugar and no chillies; that from West Java is very similar to the Sumatran one, in that it uses chillies, tomatoes and ground coconut, but it shares the laos of the Central Javanese recipe. The

94

Sumatran dish, on the other hand, is more like a Malay one with its balance of cumin and fennel. This recipe also uses peppercorns, a trade item of the area.

I. GULÉ DJAWA (Central Java)

2 lbs. lean lamb loin chops
1 lb. onions, chopped
4 cloves garlic
1 tablespoon coriander seeds
a small pinch of cumin (optional)
1 tablespoon turmeric
1 small slice green ginger
1 tablespoon laos powder
3 curry leaves
1 stalk lemon grass, bruised but not sliced
3 cloves
2-inch-piece cinnamon bark
2 cardamom pods
2 tjabé Djawa* (optional)
a pinch of mace
a few Macadamia nuts or almonds
4–5 cups coconut milk
sugar to taste
salt and pepper to taste
juice of 1 small lemon
coconut oil

In an electric blender, grind the dry seeds to a powder. Add all the other spices (including the garlic and onions), except the lemon grass and curry leaves, put in the nuts and grind everything to a paste, adding enough oil to keep the blades turning. Place a wok or a pan over a medium heat. Heat a little more oil in the pan and fry the spice paste until it no longer sticks to the sides of the

* Tjabé Djawa is a spice known only in the area which gives it its name. It tastes something like a cross between black pepper and cardamom. The dish is still recognizable without it. You can order it by mail from Mrs. De Wildt, R.F.D. 1, Bangor, Pennsylvania.

pan. Add the meat which has been cut into 2-inch strips, the curry leaves and the lemon grass and stir well. At this point check the salt, pepper and sugar content and adjust if necessary. Add the coconut milk and continue cooking *uncovered* and stirring all the while until the oil 'comes out' of the gravy. Add the lemon juice, stir again, and serve.

II. GULÉ KAMBING (Mutton Gulé) (West Java – Sundanese)

2 lbs. lamb or mutton from the leg, cubed
2 yellow onions, finely sliced
1 stalk lemon grass
1-inch-slice green ginger, smashed and chopped
4 cloves garlic, smashed and chopped
7 chillies
1 tablespoon turmeric
4 curry leaves
12 Macadamia nuts (about 2 oz.)
¾ teaspoon laos powder *or* 1 slice fresh laos (lengkuas)
7 cloves
a pinch of cumin seeds
1 tablespoon coriander seeds
¾ teaspoon nutmeg
2 sticks cinnamon bark
3 small ripe tomatoes, peeled and chopped
1 tablespoon salt
3–4 cups thick coconut milk
5 tablespoons coconut or peanut oil
½ cup grated fresh or dried coconut

Grind the coriander and cumin in a blender. Heat 1 tablespoon oil in a pan and fry the nutmeg, whole cloves and cinnamon together with the coriander and cumin. Lift out and keep aside. In another clean pan fry the grated coconut without oil until it is golden brown. Further grind it in a blender as fine as possible and keep aside.

Grind the salt, chillies, ginger, laos, half the lemon grass, the turmeric, nuts, garlic and onions in that order in the blender.

Add any oil necessary to keep the blades turning and blend to a fine paste.

Heat the pan once more and fry the oily paste until it is cooked and the spices no longer stick to the pan. Put the grated coconut in the pan with the spice mixture. Add the curry leaves and the remaining lemon grass, which has been bruised but not sliced. Add the meat and stir until it is well coated and brown. Add the tomatoes and, when they are soft, the coconut milk, and cook without a lid over a medium heat until the meat is tender (about 1 hour). Near the end of the cooking time add the fried spices. Stir them in, allow to cook a little longer, and serve.

III. GULÉ KAMBING (Mutton Gulé) (North Sumatra)

1 lb. mutton or lamb from the leg, cubed
1-inch-slice green ginger, smashed and chopped
½-inch-piece cinnamon bark
3 cloves
2 cardamom pods, broken open and half crushed
10 whole black peppercorns
⅜ teaspoon cumin seeds
⅜ teaspoon fennel seeds
1½ teaspoons coriander seeds
¾ teaspoon turmeric
7 dried chillies
1 large yellow onion, chopped
2 cloves garlic, smashed and chopped
¾ teaspoon nutmeg
3 Macadamia nuts
¾ teaspoon poppy seeds (optional)
1-inch-stalk lemon grass, bruised but not sliced
salt to taste
a squeeze of lemon or lime juice
1 large tomato, peeled and chopped
¼ cup grated fresh or dried coconut
1½–2 cups thick coconut milk
coconut or peanut oil

Heat a little oil in a pan and fry the chopped onion with the whole cloves, cinnamon, and the cardamom until soft. In an electric blender grind the rest of the dry spices to a powder. Add the garlic, ginger and Macadamia nuts, putting in a little oil if necessary to keep the blades turning, and grind to a fine paste. Add this paste to the onion mixture in the pan.

In another clean pan, fry the grated coconut without oil until it is yellow. Grind it as fine as possible and put it in the pan with the spice mixture. Put in the meat and tomatoes and fry, stirring all the time, until the meat and spices are well mixed and brown. Add the coconut milk, lemon grass and salt to taste; cover, and simmer until the meat is tender. Five minutes before the end of the cooking time, stir in the lemon juice. Adjust the seasoning and serve.

KORMAH KAMBING (Mutton Kormah)

This recipe has come to me from North Sumatra, but it is almost indistinguishable from the Kurma of Malaya. (Although the ingredients have been split up for the sake of simplicity, it is advisable to prepare all vegetables and spices before beginning step 1.)

Step I

2 lbs. lamb or mutton from the leg, cut into 1½-inch cubes
with or without bone
1 tablespoon coriander seeds
1½ teaspoons cumin seeds
1½ teaspoons fennel seeds
1½ teaspoons whole black peppercorns
2 cardamom seeds
1½ teaspoons poppy seeds (optional)
1½-inch-piece green ginger
1 yellow onion

Grind the dry spices to a powder in an electric blender or a mortar. Peel the green ginger, smash it with the flat side of a Chinese cleaver, then chop with the sharp edge of the same cleaver. Finely chop the onion. Now mix all these spices with the meat cubes and leave aside in a bowl until you are ready to use them.

Step II

1 tablespoon butter or ghee
4-inch-stick cinnamon
10 cloves
$\frac{1}{2}$ piece star anise

Heat the butter or ghee in a saucepan and fry the cinnamon, cloves and star anise *whole* for 1 minute.

Step III

10 small cloves garlic, chopped
1 yellow onion, chopped
1 stalk lemon grass, sliced fine
1 tablespoon salt

Add these to the frying spices and continue to fry until the onion is light brown. Then put in the spiced meat and stir thoroughly.

Step IV

2 cups thick coconut milk
2 large potatoes, peeled and diced

Add the coconut milk to the pan and half cook the meat (about 30 minutes). When the curry is half cooked add the diced potato, stir the pot, and cook with a lid on until both meat and potatoes are done.

This dish is good eaten with Roti Djalah (see below) instead of rice. Indonesians have it this way as a mid-morning or afternoon snack, though at proper meal times it would demand the dignity of rice.

ROTI DJALAH

This is a kind of lightly cooked pancake with holes.

4 cups sifted all-purpose flour
3 eggs
salt

Mix these ingredients with enough water to make a thin batter. Have ready on top of the stove a hot greased pan. Dip all five fingers of one hand deep into the bowl of batter and let the mixture run from your hand into the pan in a lacy pattern. Turn the pancake over before it is brown and lightly cook the other side.

DENDENG RAGI (Crisp Fried Meat) (Sumatra)

1 lb. rump steak or top round, sliced very thinly across the grain and
  cut into 2-inch squares
about ¾ cup shredded coconut just moistened with very little water
4 dried hot 'birdseye' chillies
1 tablespoon coriander seeds
2 teaspoons cumin seeds
1 small yellow onion, chopped
3 cloves garlic, smashed and chopped
10 whole black peppercorns
4 tablespoons tamarind water made from a piece of tamarind the
  size of a walnut (see p. 37)
1½ teaspoons brown sugar
salt to taste
coconut or peanut oil

Grind the chillies, coriander, cumin and peppercorns to a powder in an electric blender. Add the garlic, onion and just enough water to keep the blades turning, and grind to a paste. Put the paste in a saucepan, add the meat slices and shredded coconut, cover, and stew gently *without any extra liquid* until the meat is cooked. Uncover, add the tamarind water and cook uncovered until quite dry.

Now heat about 5 or 6 tablespoons coconut or peanut oil in a wok or pan and fry the contents of the saucepan, turning them about occasionally, until the meat is crisp and yellow. This will take anything up to 1 hour. Drain on paper toweling. Serve with rice and a vegetable dish.

Vegetables and Salads

Indonesian vegetable dishes assume one of four main forms known respectively as Sajur, Tumis, Gulé, and a group one can only loosely call salad. I have placed most of the Sajur group in the soup section, though they are more authentically vegetable dishes, and could just as easily be included here.

SAJUR LEMENG

This is a kind of vegetable, white curry not unlike the Indian Avial.

1 lb. vegetables of various kinds, sliced or shredded (green beans or broad beans, pumpkin, cabbage, eggplant, canned bamboo shoots or zucchini)
4 dried hot chillies
$\frac{3}{4}$ teaspoon or $\frac{1}{2}$-inch-slice trasi (shrimp paste)
2 small yellow onions, chopped
3 cloves garlic, smashed and chopped
5 Macadamia nuts
1$\frac{1}{2}$ teaspoons coriander seeds
$\frac{1}{4}$ cup shredded or dried grated coconut, moistened
$\frac{1}{4}$ lb. peeled shrimp
salt to taste
1 cup thick coconut milk.

In an electric blender grind the coriander, chillies, Macadamia nuts, trasi, garlic and onion in that order, adding oil towards the end to allow the blades to turn. Heat a wok or a saucepan and fry the spice paste until it is cooked. Add the coconut milk, the vegetables that take longer to cook, the shredded coconut and shrimp, and allow to simmer. Add the faster-cooking vegetables a little later and simmer, stirring, until all the vegetables are cooked and the gravy thick, its oil having 'come out.'

TUMIS (Stir-fried Vegetable)

½ lb. vegetable of any kind (for instance, shredded cabbage, zucchini, sliced fresh beans, very young peas in the pod)
1 clove garlic, smashed and chopped
1 yellow onion, finely sliced
2 fresh chillies, finely sliced, seeds removed
2 curry leaves
1 teaspoon laos powder (lengkuas)
1 stem lemon grass, finely sliced
salt to taste
a dash of dark soya sauce
¼ cup coconut or peanut oil

Heat the oil in a wok or a pan and fry the onions, garlic, chillies, laos, lemon grass and curry leaves until soft. Add the vegetable and stir-fry until it is lightly cooked but still crisp. Add a dash of soya sauce and salt to taste, stir again and serve.

If you live in the tropics, try tumis using shredded green pawpaw and raw peanuts. It is an especially good combination.

SAMBAL GORENG SAJURAN
(Chilli-fried Vegetable)

1 lb. vegetable (cabbage, green beans, or new potato are the favourites) *or* soya bean curd, diced
1 tablespoon ground chilli powder
2 yellow onions, chopped
3 cloves garlic, smashed and chopped
1½ teaspoons laos powder
coconut or peanut oil
1½ teaspoons trasi *or* 1-inch-slice hard trasi (shrimp paste)
3 curry leaves
1½ teaspoons sugar
salt to taste
1–2 tablespoons tamarind water made from a walnut-sized piece of tamarind (see p. 37)
2 cups thick coconut milk

In an electric blender grind the chilli, laos, trasi, garlic and onions to a smooth paste, adding sufficient coconut oil or peanut oil to keep the machine working. Heat a wok, add the spice paste and fry until it is well brown and aromatic. Add the coconut milk, curry leaves and sugar, stir and add the vegetable. Simmer, uncovered, until the vegetable is cooked. Then add the tamarind water and salt to taste, and stir until the gravy is thick and dark.

The Sumatran version of this dish would use 2 ripe tomatoes, chopped, instead of the tamarind water. These would be fried after the spices are soft, before adding the coconut milk. No sugar would be added to the recipe, and the trasi would be optional.

GULÉ PAKIS (Vegetable Gulé) (Sumatra)

1 lb. broccoli
a few small dried fish, washed, their heads removed* (optional)
4 Macadamia nuts
1-inch-slice green ginger, smashed and chopped
¾ teaspoon turmeric
1 tablespoon or more ground chilli
1 large yellow onion, chopped
2 cloves garlic (optional)
1-inch-stem lemon grass, bruised (optional)
2½ cups thick coconut milk
2 or 3 basil leaves
salt to taste
juice of 1 lemon

Wash and slice the broccoli. In an electric blender grind together the nuts, chillies, turmeric, ginger, garlic and onions. Add the coconut milk and blend well. Put the resulting broth into a wide pan or wok, add the lemon grass and basil, dried fish and lemon juice and bring to the boil.

Boil the gravy fast without a lid, stirring all the time, until it

* These can be obtained from Chinese groceries.

reduces and thickens. Put in the broccoli and continue to boil, uncovered, until the vegetable is cooked and the oil has 'come out' of the gravy. Adjust salt and serve.

TAHU GORENG KETJAP
(Fried Bean Curd with Soya Sauce)

6 squares soya bean curd
oil for deep frying
¼ lb. bean sprouts, scalded
1 green cucumber with skin, sliced
5 tablespoons dark soya sauce
2 cloves garlic, smashed and chopped
1 tablespoon finely chopped onion
1 fresh hot chilli, finely chopped
sugar to taste
freshly squeezed lemon juice
chopped celery and fried onion flakes for garnish

Cut the soya bean curd into 1-inch cubes and deep-fry until brown and crisp on the outside. Arrange on a plate. Cover with bean sprouts and cucumber. Combine the soya sauce, garlic, onion, chilli, sugar and lemon juice in an electric blender and mix thoroughly. Pour this sauce over the vegetables. Garnish with chopped celery and fried onion flakes and serve.

ATJAR TJAMPUR ATAU KUNING
(Mixed Pickled Vegetable)

about 1 lb. raw vegetables in the following proportions:
    ¼ lb. green beans, cut into 1-inch lengths
    ¼ lb. shredded cabbage
    ¼ lb. carrots, cut into matchstick lengths
    1 oz. cauliflower flowerets
    ½ small cucumber with skin, seeds removed and sliced
2 or 3 whole fresh chillies, seeds removed
½-inch-piece green ginger, sliced

1 or 2 cloves garlic, smashed and chopped
¾ teaspoon turmeric
coconut or peanut oil
½ cup water
4 Macadamia nuts
1 tablespoon or less white sugar, according to taste
1 stalk lemon grass, bruised (optional)
¼ cup white vinegar

Slice the onions finely. Grind the garlic and turmeric and rub them into a paste. Heat a little coconut oil or peanut oil and fry the onion slices until they are golden. Add the paste and fry until it is cooked. Add the chillies, each sliced into thirds, the vinegar, sugar, ginger slices, lemon grass and 1 cup water. Put in the vegetables and stir until the sauce thickens a little and the vegetables are lightly cooked.

GADO-GADO (Cooked Vegetable Salad)

bean sprouts, blanched
green beans cut into 1-inch lengths very lightly boiled
finely shredded cabbage, blanched
soya bean curd, cubed and deep fried in peanut oil until brown and
  crisp on the outside
new potatoes, boiled and sliced
young carrots, sliced lengthwise and lightly cooked
1 green cucumber with skin intact, cut into thick strips
1 hard-boiled egg, peeled and halved or sliced

Arrange the vegetables in layers on a flat plate – first the potatoes, then green beans, carrots, bean curd, cucumber, bean sprouts, cabbage and egg. Pour over the following sauce.

Gado-Gado sauce

3 cloves garlic, smashed and chopped
1 teaspoon trasi (blachan, shrimp paste) *or* 1-inch-square-slice hard
  trasi
7 fresh chillies, seeds removed

106

½ lb. raw peanuts *or* ½-lb. jar crunchy peanut butter
¾ teaspoon laos powder (lengkuas) *or* 1 slice fresh laos
2 curry leaves
1 tablespoon brown sugar (or less according to taste)
2 cups thick coconut milk
2 tablespoons coconut oil
1½ teaspoons lemon juice or white vinegar

If you are using raw peanuts, fry them in a smear of oil until they are cooked. Remove and keep aside.

Heat the rest of the oil in the pan and fry separately and in that order the whole chillies, the garlic and the trasi. In an electric blender grind the chillies, garlic and trasi finely, then add the peanuts and grind roughly. Add the coconut milk and sugar and blend thoroughly. Transfer the mixture into a saucepan, add the laos powder and curry leaves, bring to the boil and cook until the sauce thickens a little. It should remain of pouring consistency; if necessary, add water to achieve this. Take the sauce off the fire, add the lemon juice or vinegar, stir, and pour over the vegetables. Garnish with finely chopped celery, and fried onion flakes or chopped green onions.

Another dish called Lotek consists of the same vegetables and sauce, but everything is tossed together and eaten straight away.

PETJEL (Cooked Vegetable Salad and Uncooked Sauce)

Small separate heaps of lightly cooked vegetables – shredded cabbage, very young spinach, sliced potato, halved hard-boiled eggs – are arranged on a plate, and served accompanied by Petjel Sauce in a separate bowl. Guests help themselves to vegetables and sauce.

Petjel sauce

¼ cup fried peanuts roughly ground *or* 3 tablespoons crunchy peanut butter
¾ teaspoon ground chilli powder

¼ clove garlic, smashed and chopped
½ yellow onion, finely chopped
¾ teaspoon trasi fried in foil (see p. 28)
1½ teaspoons brown sugar
5 tablespoons water

Combine all the sauce ingredients in a blender and mix thoroughly.

ASINAN (Raw Vegetable Salad)

Place some washed raw bean sprouts, shredded cabbage and strips of cucumber complete with skin in a salad bowl. Toss with a dressing made from white vinegar, a little white sugar to taste, a few dried shrimp fried first and then ground, salt and chilli powder to taste. The dressing should be thin and sour.

For a party, place the tossed mixture on a bed of lettuce leaves and sprinkle roughly ground roasted peanuts over the top.

RUDJAK

Rudjak is a dish which figures large in the Javanese list of special foods for ritual occasions. It is served, for instance, at the *slametan* (celebration) which precedes the birth of a first child.

A lot of argument usually accompanies the decision whether to propose rudjak as a salad or a sweet. I have chosen to place it here because of the savoury nature of its dressing, and also because rudjak can be made either with fruit, as in the recipe, or with the usual Indonesian salad vegetables.

1 lb. mixed fruit and vegetables (sliced cucumber, diced pineapple,
   orange or grapefruit segments, pawpaw, green mangoes
   or apple slices)
2 chopped 'birdseye' chillies
¾ teaspoon trasi (blachan) *or* ½-inch by ½-inch-slice hard trasi, fried
   in foil (see p. 28)

1 tablespoon brown sugar
1 tablespoon fish sauce (available from Chinese groceries but
    optional)
1 tablespoon lemon juice
a little water

Combine the chillies, trasi, sugar, fish sauce, lemon juice and water in an electric blender and mix thoroughly. Toss with the fruit and allow to stand for a while before serving.

URAP

½ lb. or more mixed lightly cooked vegetables (beans sliced in 1-inch
    lengths, scalded bean sprouts, diced celery)
½ fresh coconut, brown skin removed, flesh grated
¾ teaspoon cooked trasi (blachan)
2 fresh hot chillies, finely sliced
brown sugar to taste
salt to taste
½ clove garlic, smashed and chopped

Mix the coconut, garlic, sugar, salt and spices together. Allow to stand for a few minutes, then toss with the vegetables until well mixed. Serve straight away. If you intend to keep any of this dish overnight, the grated coconut needs to be steamed before it is used.

Egg Dishes and Patties

SAMBAL GORENG TELOR (Chilli-fried Eggs)

6 hard-boiled eggs, peeled
1 tablespoon sambal oelek *or* 1 tablespoon ground chilli
1½ yellow onions, chopped
3 cloves garlic, smashed and chopped
¾ teaspoon laos powder (lengkuas)
1½ stalks lemon grass, finely sliced
3 curry leaves
2 Macadamia nuts (optional)
1½ teaspoons salt
1½ teaspoons brown sugar
1½ cups coconut milk
coconut or peanut oil

In an electric blender combine the chilli, nuts, onions and garlic and grind to a paste, adding just enough oil to keep the machine turning. Heat a wok or pan on the stove and fry the spices until they are well browned and aromatic. Add the coconut milk, brown sugar, salt, laos, lemon grass and curry leaves and allow to boil. Put in the whole eggs and continue to cook without a lid, stirring all the time until the sauce reduces and thickens and the oil 'comes out.'

PINDANG TELOR (Spiced Eggs)

6 hard-boiled eggs
½ yellow onion, finely chopped
2 cloves garlic, smashed and chopped
¾ teaspoon laos
1 stem lemon grass, bruised (optional)
¾ cup water
1 tablespoon coconut oil

Peel and lightly score the eggs with a fork. Mash the onions and garlic together in a mortar. Heat the oil in a wok and fry the onions and garlic until soft. Add the laos, lemon grass and about ¾ cup water and allow to simmer. Put in the whole eggs and allow to simmer, stirring, about 10 minutes. The water should have evaporated by now, its flavours having delicately penetrated the eggs.

DADAR DJAWA (Javanese Omelette)

4 eggs
½ yellow onion, finely chopped
2 hot chillies, finely sliced
1 tablespoon Javanese soya sauce (see p. 36) *or* 2 teaspoons dark
  soya sauce plus 1 teaspoon brown sugar
2 tablespoons peanut oil

Lightly beat the eggs with a little water, salt and the Javanese soya sauce. Heat the oil in a pan, fry the onions and chillies until soft. Pour in the egg and allow it to half set. Then either run channels through it gently with the flat tip of a knife or a pair of chopsticks, or lift the edges of the setting omelette and tilt the pan so that the remaining liquid comes into contact with the hot pan. The aim of these processes is to set all the egg in the omelette. The whole must end up in one unbroken piece. When completely set, allow to fry until the omelette is golden brown on the bottom. Ease out of the pan on to a plate and serve.

TAHU PONG (Bean Curd Omelette)

3 cakes soya bean curd
2 eggs
1 tablespoon Javanese soya sauce (see p. 36) *or* 1 tablespoon dark
  soya sauce plus 1 tablespoon brown sugar
1 tablespoon crunchy peanut butter

Chop the bean curd roughly and drain it through a sieve. Beat the eggs lightly. Heat a little peanut oil in a frying pan and pour

111

in the eggs mixed with the bean curd. Fry as an omelette until golden brown. In the meantime combine the soya sauce and peanut butter in an electric blender. Lift out the omelette, pour the sauce over the top, and serve.

BÉGEDEL DJAGUNG (Sweet Corn Patties)

About 1½ cups frozen or canned sweet corn kernels
2 tablespoons finely chopped onion
1 clove garlic, smashed and chopped
2 tablespoons finely chopped celery
salt and pepper to taste
2 fresh chillies, finely sliced (optional)
1 egg, beaten
1 tablespoon plain flour
1 tablespoon cake flour

Mix all the ingredients together, adding a little water if necessary to form a batter. Grease an electric frying pan or a heavy griddle and drop spoonfuls of the mixture on to it. Fry on both sides till brown.

Bégedel Djagung is very good with ⅜ lb. of chopped cooked shrimp added to the batter mixture. In this case, use 4 teaspoons of each type of flour and a little more water. Otherwise proceed as above.

BÉGEDEL GORENG (Fried Patties)

1 lb. potato, boiled and mashed
½ lb. ground beef
¼ cup finely sliced onion
salt and pepper to taste
1½ teaspoons nutmeg
2 eggs
peanut oil

Heat a little oil in a frying pan and fry the beef until it changes colour. Lift out and mix with the mashed potato. Put in a little more oil and fry the onions until light brown. Remove and mash in a mortar with the nutmeg, salt and pepper. Beat the eggs. Mix the spices, meat and potato together in a bowl. Add the eggs and mix thoroughly. Now spoon on to a greased hot griddle and fry on both sides until brown. Serve with Serundeng (see p. 115) sprinkled over the top.

REMPAH (Meat and Coconut Patties)

½ lb. ground beef
½ coconut, grated, *or* ½ cup dried grated coconut, moistened
1 clove garlic, smashed and chopped
¾ teaspoon coriander, ground
a pinch of cumin, ground
1 small egg
coconut oil for frying

Combine all the ingredients in a bowl and mix well. Shape into small patties and shallow fry turning once until brown on both sides. Rempah can be served with Nasi Kuning (see p. 48) or on their own as hamburgers.

Sambals and Garnishes

SAMBAL KELAPA (Coconut Sambal)

½ young fresh coconut *or* ½ cup dried grated coconut, moistened
1 fresh red chilli, finely chopped
⅜ teaspoon trasi (blachan) fried in foil (see p. 28)
1 citrus (lemon or orange) leaf *or* a squeeze of lemon juice
a very little sugar
salt to taste
1½ teaspoons finely chopped onion (optional)
½ clove garlic, smashed and chopped (optional)

Remove the brown skin from the coconut and grate it finely, if you are using the fresh. Mix all the ingredients together well and allow to stand for a while before serving.

SAMBAL BUBUK DARI KATJANG
(Mashed Peanut Sambal)

2–4 oz. raw peanuts
¾ teaspoon trasi (blachan)
1 fresh hot chilli
½ citrus leaf
a little sugar (optional)
salt to taste

Dry-fry the peanuts in a heavy pan until they are cooked. Wrap the trasi in foil and dry-fry it, then remove the foil wrapper. Put everything into a blender and grind together until they are mashed and well mixed.

SAMBALS WHICH WILL KEEP

There are a number of favourite Indonesian sambals which are readily available commercially in small jars. They are produced by various Dutch and Indonesian firms and are to be found in most large American cities.* They include Sambal Oelek, Sambal Badjak, Sambal Peteh, and Sambal Goreng Ebbi. Since these keep indefinitely, particularly if refrigerated, I think it is a better proposition to buy them ready-made than to fiddle with small quantities yourself. They are spooned in *very* minute quantities on to the side of the plate and eaten as a condiment with rice and other main dishes. Beginners must be warned that these sambals are only for the brave!

SERUNDENG (Peanut-Coconut Garnish)

1½ cups dried grated coconut
1½ teaspoons ground cumin
1 tablespoon brown sugar
1 medium yellow onion, finely chopped
2 cloves garlic, smashed and chopped
½-inch-slice green ginger, smashed and chopped
1 tablespoon tamarind water (see p. 37) or lemon juice
4–6 oz. roasted peanuts

Mix the coconut, cumin, sugar, onion, garlic, ginger and tamarind water together. Smear a heavy frying pan with oil and fry the mixture over a very low heat, stirring all the time, until it is golden brown. Allow to cool, mix in the roasted peanuts, and serve.

ATJAR KETIMUN (Cucumber Pickle)

6 medium cucumbers
3 hot chillies
salt to taste
3 cups white vinegar
5 tablespoons sugar

* You can also order sambals by mail from Mrs. De Wildt, R.F.D. 1, Bangor, Pennsylvania,

Wash the cucumbers and remove the seeds, but do not peel them. Cut them into small dice. Slice the chillies and mix with the cucumbers. Add salt and leave aside for an hour, then drain off any excess water. Mix the sugar and vinegar together and heat them until the sugar dissolves. Allow to cool, pour over the cucumber and serve. If you wish to store the pickle in jars, put the cucumber and chilli mixture into the boiling syrup, return to the boil, then remove from the fire. Pour into clean jars, allow to cool, and cover.

KRUPUK (Shrimp Crisp)

Krupuk is a large crispy slice made from a batter of dried shrimp and tapioca. Even in Indonesia, it is bought already processed and only needs to be deep-fried and drained just before serving. In many gourmet shops and Asian stores – as well as from various mail-order sources – you can buy the authentic large krupuk, but if this is not available the common Chinese small shrimp crisps are a suitable substitute. It is served with any rice meal and eaten as a sort of bread.

Malaysia and Singapore

A LL the flavours of South East Asia, social as well as culinary, are concentrated in Malaysia and Singapore. The ethnic, historical and cultural elements that lie beneath the surface of any South East Asian country here become strikingly evident. The population is remarkably diverse: in 1960, 47 per cent were Malays, 42 per cent were Chinese, and the remaining 11 per cent consisted of Indians, Dyaks and others.* And though you may not get an impression of variety from Singapore alone, which is a predominantly Chinese island-city, the several pots bubble steadily in other parts of Malaysia.

Such a situation may at times cause disturbances in the nation's political life, but it can only throw the diner into ecstasy. For here you have in one geographical area three separate, well-defined styles of cookery, each reflecting its own distinct cultural and religious influences.

The food of the Malays is very similar to that of their relatives, the Indonesians. Indeed, many well-known Malay dishes such as Dondeng, Rendang, or Opor will not be found in this part of the book, as I have already dealt with them in my chapter on Indonesian food. The reasons for this similarity are historical. Long before the modern national boundaries as we know them were set by colonial administrations, much of Sumatra and Malaya and possibly parts of Borneo were first joined loosely together in the Kingdom of Srivijaja. These areas saw considerable movements of people, and must also have had other contacts with each other since the life of Srivijaja was based on trade. So it is natural that they should have enjoyed dishes in common for many centuries.

What differences there are between Malay and Indonesian food also have their roots in historical and geographical con-

*I have taken these figures from the period before Singapore's separation from Malaysia, as the two are being dealt with together here.

ditions. Indonesian food as a whole represents an amalgam of the somewhat separate Javanese and Sumatran/outer island traditions: the first is the food of an elaborate agricultural world, deeply colonized, using the products of that world; the second is influenced by the trade on which the Sumatran/outer island economies were largely based, showing a greater use of dry seeds and dry aromatic spices. This makes the typical Sumatran/outer island dish a more complex 'curry,' though of course at its edges modern Sumatran cooking reflects some Javanese characteristics, and vice-versa.

Malay dishes are more uniform. The distinctively 'agrarian' element, if there ever was one, has given way almost completely to the second tradition, which is the overpowering one in Malaya. It is only quite recent migrations of the late nineteenth and early twentieth centuries that have brought an imported Javanese 'nona-style' of cooking to Malaya.

Chinese food, of course, needs no introduction. You will find in Malaysia and Singapore any of the different regional styles of cooking of mainland China. Often, perhaps, the original dish is given a local flavour by the addition of the inevitable side-dish of chilli sauce, sliced chilli in vinegar, or even by the use of fresh red chilli to garnish the food, but in the main, the Chinese heritage remains intact. I have merely provided a tiny selection here.

The exception to the rule is the Straits Chinese style, and if you are interested in defining a distinctively 'South East Asian' style of cookery, it is also the most fascinating element in Malaysian Chinese food. Straits Chinese dishes usually contain a mixture of Chinese ingredients (pork for instance, which is not eaten by the Moslem Malays) cooked in a Malay manner.

The separate strain of Straits Chinese food came into existence in a rather romantic way. The Straits Chinese are descended from people born in Malacca and Penang, particularly the latter, after the foundation of Penang as the first British settlement of Malaya.* The British deliberately encouraged Chinese immigra-

*See Victor Purcell: *The Chinese in Malaya*, Oxford University Press, 1948.

118

tion, seeing Chinese industriousness as a source of wealth and revenue for the colony. By the mid-nineteenth century Penang had become a real Chinese city based on trade and sugar cultivation, the merchants eventually building their trade on the importation of coolie labour from China. About the 1830s and '40s, the Straits-born Chinese, descended from the early arrivals, began to appear, conditioned very much by local influences, and not yet swamped in numbers by the China-born immigrants. They saw themselves as apart from the immigrants, as indeed they were, being British subjects. They were in the main brought up as Chinese, steeped in the Chinese heritage. But there was one important difference: they usually had Malay or half-caste mothers. The Chinese Government in the early days had restricted the emigration of women to Malaya, and the immigrants at this time took local wives. This meant that the cooking was heavily Malay-influenced, a fitting reminder that love and food go together. And so it remains in Straits Chinese families even today, though in religion and culture they do not stand noticeably apart.

The Indian community in Malaya is much smaller than the Malay or Chinese, but within its bounds there is a fascinating variety of groups and styles of cooking that carry over from all the regions of India and from Ceylon. Where it has been possible to do so I have noted the locality from which a recipe is said to come, so that anyone who is interested can identify the subtle differences in flavour and food habit associated with the various areas.

Most numerous are the South Indian Tamil and Telugu people who make up the bulk of the largest Indian social group in Malaya – the plantation workers and unskilled labourers. South Indians are well known as rice-eaters, and their food is generally simple. Their curries are hotter than those in the north, but not so rich. Gravies are thin with a liberal addition of coconut milk, and vegetarian dishes are more common than meat. When meat dishes do occur, they are usually of mutton or chicken, never, of course, of beef which is anathema to Hindus.

The Indian business community in Malaya is one of mixed

origin: Gujerati merchants, both Hindu and Moslem; South Indian Moslems (Marakkayars); a few Sikh businessmen; and Chettiars from South India. The North Indian and Moslem recipes that one comes across in Malaya probably originate within this group. These dishes are distinguished by the use of richer ingredients – ghee, yoghurt, cinnamon, and the 'black' spices, cloves, pepper, and cardamoms, wheat-flour preparations and more meat dishes.

There is, too, a small group of Ceylon and Jaffna Tamils, descendants of early merchants from Ceylon who came to Malaya along with the British. According to one authority it is not only their food that sets this group a little apart from other Indian groups in Malaya, but also the fact that they have less political contact with India and remain to this day a source of silent tension within the Indian community with whom they are grouped for political purposes.*

But to my mind Ceylon Tamil food *does* stand out as distinct from the food of India itself. It has been more influenced by Sinhalese cooking, and uses more of the blend of uncooked aromatic ingredients associated with South East Asian food than those of the Indian mainland – lemon grass, for instance, curry leaves and fennel, dried shrimp preparations and coconut milk. Not far removed from the South Indian practice, it is true, but a shade closer, I think, to the South East Asian style.

Whatever the subtle and not so subtle differences between communal forms of eating in Malaysia, they do share one important basic food. Since nobody lives very far away from the coast or from rivers almost anywhere in the more densely settled areas of the country, *fish* assumes a position of considerable importance in the diet of most groups. And it is precisely at this point that confusion and bewilderment have clouded the appreciation of Malaysian cooking among foreigners. Seldom is any effort made to translate Malay fish into a recognizable foreign equivalent, the usual assumption being that it is impossible anyway and people might as well hit or miss with any fish they

*Usha Mahajani: *The Role of Indian Minorities in Burma and Malaya*, Vora and Co., Bombay, 1960.

like. I think, however, that an attempt in this direction can and should be made.

American fish

American fish are naturally enough quite different from those found in South East Asia and it is impossible to lay down exact equivalents in taste and texture between the two. However, the following substitutes, based mainly on common ways of cooking the fish in the United States, produce good results. Specific suggestions are also given in the recipes.

For broiling and frying use haddock, cod, hake, sole, flounder, fluke, mullet, sea bass or pollock. Most of these can also be steamed.

For curries, cod, mullet, mackerel, tuna, pompano, ocean perch, salmon, and even eels seem to suggest themselves.

For roasting or broiling over charcoal using a coconut milk sauce, I should try herring, whiting, haddock, halibut, shad, salmon or trout.

Here is a short glossary of the more common Malaysian fish and their American counterparts, where I have been able to identify them. Such a list may be of help to people who come across Malaysian recipes by other means where there is no guide to their use overseas.

Ikan merah	Snapper, porgy, ocean perch, blackfish
Kurau, Selangin or Senangin	Salmon
Kerapu	Ocean perch
Belanak	Mullet
Bawal puteh	Pompano
Bawal tambah, Bawal hitam	Blue runner
Bulus-bulus	King whiting

121

Baji	Scorpion fish
Kembong	Small bonito or tuna
Ikan ayer	Tuna
Selar	King mackerel
Tenggiri	Pacific mackerel, Spanish mackerel
Selayar	Escolar, snake mackerel
Ikan todak	Pike

When it comes to serving Malaysian food, I have often been asked two types of question. First, how many dishes do you serve at one time and what sorts of combinations should they represent? Secondly, do you stick to the style of one community at each meal, or can you combine Malay, Chinese and Indian?

On the first question, the local practice here is more or less the same as with meals in other countries of South East Asia. On the dinner table you present about four or five separate dishes with rice and condiments – say a selection from a fish dish, a shrimp one, a meat, a vegetable, a chicken or duck, a salad, and a soup. They are all served in large central bowls, and each person has an individual plate, spoon and fork, and a small soup bowl. The diner helps himself to whatever he wants when he wants it. You can pile your plate with a serving from each central dish, or take one at a time, according to taste, but it is not really considered polite to take too much at one time. The Chinese practice is to drink soup last in order to cleanse the mouth, but Malays and Indonesians take dips from their soup at the same time as other dishes. Main courses are usually followed by fresh fruit, not pudding, the more complex sweets and cakes being reserved for between-meal snacks which are very popular among the better-off.

All that has been said roughly applies to Chinese family meals as well as to the others, but on special occasions the Chinese meal becomes a banquet, with each dish being brought on separately, after the one before has been completely finished and time for resting and toasting allowed. The Chinese banquet is a complicated matter with its own rituals, and I have not attempted to deal with it in these pages.

For the Anglo-Saxon family meal, and certainly for the beginner, I suggest that it is better to stick to one or two dishes with rice, served in a larger quantity than the amounts that would be allowed if the table were more heavily laden. That is why most of the recipes here have been calculated to serve two people if there is only one dish to be served, or six if there are four or five. Branch out into authenticity only if you have guests and are intent on impressing, for preparing a proper Asian meal is a time- and anxiety-consuming process especially in Western countries where one does not have servants and has to hunt for ingredients.

As to the second question, I do not recommend mixing your food styles, unless you are very well acquainted with the flavours of various Asian foods. This is sometimes done in Malaya, particularly by Indians and Malays, whose cookery shows a more common tradition, but on the whole it is not regularly practised. I do at times serve a mixture of Indonesian, Malay, Ceylon and Indian curries, but you really have to know in advance that the finished products are likely to blend successfully, and this is very much a matter of experience.

At the end of this chapter, I have included a section of 'Miscellaneous Malaysian' recipes. In a multi-racial country like Malaysia, particularly in the cities, you get people of all kinds who do not see themselves as members of a firmly-rooted group and who freely borrow and adapt all sorts of methods of flavouring food. In the 'Miscellaneous Malaysian' section you will find recipes like this, together with those where I have for some reason been doubtful about the origins of the dish. But the reader is warned not to expect that dishes from this group will necessarily be easier to prepare than those that have gone before. However, once a Westerner acquires the habit of cooking Asian-style, it quickly becomes evident that many previously 'foreign' dishes are much easier to produce than a lot of our own fare. With these words of encouragement, I leave the cook to dabble.

123

Malay

OTAK-OTAK

Steamed in a large pyrex dish, Otak-otak makes an interesting savoury custard for lunch with salad or plain rice. Allow it to cool, and you have an excellent sandwich or canapé spread. But Otak-otak really appears at its best when it has been wrapped into small single-serve sealed parcels of foil (banana leaf ideally!) before cooking and thrown over a barbecue to roast and set. The packets can be opened and their contents eaten hot, or they can be stored for a day or two in the refrigerator and sent out on summer picnics.

1½ lbs. fish (cod, King mackerel, Spanish mackerel, mullet)
10 fresh chillies
4 cloves garlic
2 stalks lemon grass
10 Macadamia nuts
1 tablespoon turmeric
1 large yellow onion
1 thick slice ginger
6 lemon or lime leaves
2 teaspoons sugar
2 eggs
a dash of pepper
salt
2 tablespoons tamarind water (see p. 37)
2 cups thick coconut milk

Clean the fish and flake off the flesh. Put the chillies, onion, garlic, ginger and Macadamia nuts through the fine blade of a grinder or mash them in a blender; add the turmeric, lemon grass, finely sliced, and pound all these ingredients into a fine hash in a mortar. Slice the lemon leaves very fine. Beat the eggs.

Now put the fish, hashed spices, coconut milk, beaten eggs,

salt, sugar, tamarind water and lemon leaves in a bowl and beat together until they are thoroughly mixed. Pour the mixture into a covered pyrex dish, place it in a pan containing a little water and steam for about 30 minutes in a moderate oven. Alternatively, wrap small quantities in foil parcels and grill over a charcoal fire for a few minutes. Serve each helping in its foil wrapper.

PANGGANG IKAN BAWAL (Barbecued Flatfish)

This is a style of cooking that is very common in Malaya and Indonesia, and the result is always as delicious as the recipe suggests it will be. Anyone who believes that all Asian food is 'curry' needs only to be presented with a Panggang dish and a South East Asian salad to be quickly disabused of this idea.

1 small fish per person (dab, flounder, sole, fluke, blackback; otherwise
    blue runner)
juice of $\frac{1}{4}$ lemon

Marinade for each fish

1 yellow onion
1 clove garlic
2–3 fresh red chillies
$\frac{1}{2}$ cup thick coconut milk

Chop the onion, garlic and chillies finely, and mix them with the coconut milk. Clean and scale the fish. Make a few cuts in the skin, and marinate the fish in the spiced coconut milk for several hours. Broil over a charcoal fire or under the broiler, basting frequently with the marinade which in the meantime has been warming on the stove. When the fish is done, put it on a plate and squeeze over a little lemon juice.

STUFFED FISH MALAY-STYLE

There is a traditional Malay method of stuffing whole fish for frying or broiling which demands great skill and patience on the part of the cook. The entrails and flesh and bones are first loosened by carefully massaging the fish all over and are then removed through the gill holes. The flesh is flaked, mixed with various spices, and then stuffed back inside the uncut fish skin ready for frying. Though the result is extremely tasty, it is not a dish to be embarked upon lightly. For this reason, and because I have already included the Indonesian version of the same thing (see recipe for Saté Bandeng p. 67), I am not tempted to repeat it here.

The recipes which follow are very modern, technically simplified adaptations. I wrote down the first one from a weekly Malay-language cooking demonstration on a Penang television programme. The demonstrator was a Malay talking to Malays, but the recipe can truly be called Malaysian, its inspiration being Chinese.

IKAN BERINTI 1 (Stuffed Round Fish)

1 whole fish ungutted, about 4 lbs. (trout, large mullet, King
    mackerel, Spanish mackerel, pollock, pompano)
20 small shrimp, shelled and deveined
4 water chestnuts
¼ lb. finely ground beef
2 yellow onions
1 slice green ginger
1 teaspoon cornstarch
vegetable oil
2 tablespoons tomato sauce
a dash of soya sauce
sugar and salt to taste
chopped green leaves of green onion and chopped leafy celery
    stalks for garnish

Slice the whole fish down the *back* close to the bone and on both sides of it. Sever the bone at each end, lift out the whole bone and entrails of the fish, and discard. If you buy the fish already cleaned, you will probably have to use a front opening, when it will be harder to remove the whole backbone.

Put 1 onion, the shrimp, ginger and water chestnuts through the fine blade of a grinder, mix them well with the ground beef, and stuff this mixture back into the fish. Coat the whole thing thicky with cornstarch and fry it in plenty of hot vegetable oil until it is cooked.

In the meantime prepare the sauce. First slice the remaining onion into thick rounds. Heat about 1 tablespoon oil in a small pan and fry the onion until it is golden but not soft. Then add the tomato sauce, soya sauce, salt, sugar and cornstarch, stirring well to blend them together. Let the sauce come to boiling point and thicken, adding water if necessary to adjust the consistency. Just before serving place the whole fish on a large platter, pour the sauce over the top, and garnish with green onion leaves and celery.

IKAN BERINTI II

This second recipe for stuffing fish is more suited to a fish that has been bought already gutted and has a stomach opening.

1 large mullet, King mackerel, Spanish mackerel, or pompano
2 hot red chillies
1½ yellow onions
1½ teaspoons ground coriander
3 2-inch stalks lemon grass
1¼ teaspoons turmeric
1 tablespoon freshly grated coconut flesh *or* dried grated coconut,
    moistened in water
strips of green cucumber and fried onion flakes for garnish

Clean and scale the fish. Make three slits on each side right through to the stomach cavity and wipe dry. Chop all the stuffing ingredients and mix into a paste. Fill the cavity and slits of the fish. Fry in plenty of hot oil until crisp and brown.

Serve garnished with green cucumber strips and fried onion flakes.

GULAI IKAN (Basic Fish Curry)

1 lb. fish steaks (cod, mullet, salmon, eels, mackerel, or pompano)
2 tablespoons coriander seeds
1 teaspoon fennel seeds
¾ teaspoon cumin seeds
2 yellow onions, finely chopped
1 clove garlic, crushed
3 or 4 dried hot chillies
½-inch-piece green ginger, smashed and chopped
¾ teaspoon turmeric
1 stem lemon grass, smashed
a piece of tamarind about the size of a pea, softened in water
½ cup thick coconut milk
½–1 cup thin coconut milk, depending on how much gravy is
    preferred (the curry is best when thick)
salt to taste

Grind all the dried spices to a powder in a blender. Then put in
the onions, garlic, green ginger, and thick coconut milk, and
grind everything together into a paste. Transfer into a saucepan,
add the lemon grass and bring the mixture to the boil over a
medium fire. Lower the heat and let the pot simmer, stirring for
about 10 minutes. Then add the thin coconut milk, tamarind,
and salt to taste, raise the heat once more, stir well, and bring to
the boil. When it is bubbling, put in the fish and continue to cook
for another 5 minutes.

GULAI TUMIS (Sour Fish Curry)

2 fish steaks (cod, mullet, mackerel, salmon, or pompano)
12 dried chillies
2 stalks lemon grass, finely sliced
2 medium yellow onions, finely chopped and the excess moisture
    squeezed out
1½ teaspoons blachan (shrimp paste)

2 teaspoons turmeric
2 teaspoons lengkuas *or* laos powder
3 small cloves garlic
1¼ cups tamarind water
a few green beans, cut into 2-inch pieces
salt to taste
vegetable oil

Chop all the spices, garlic and onions together into a fine paste. Heat 2 tablespoons of vegetable oil in a wok or a frying pan and fry the spices until they are cooked and no longer stick to the pan. Add the beans and stir-fry them for about 3 minutes, then pour in the tamarind water, stirring everything together until it is well mixed. Turn down the heat. Finally, put in the fish steaks and cook for about 8 minutes, or until tender.

SAMBAL IKAN (Whole Fish Sambal)

1 whole mullet or other suitable fish (about 1½ lbs.), de-scaled and
    gutted
cornstarch
1 cup thick coconut milk
3 lime leaves
enough coconut oil or ghee to shallow-fry the fish
peanut oil
2 yellow onions
1½ teaspoons turmeric
1 tablespoon coriander seeds
¾ teaspoon fennel seeds
¾ teaspoon mustard seeds
10 fresh hot chillies (red) *or* 8 dried chillies

Make a 3- or 4-inch slit to the bone across each side of the fish and rub its skin lightly with cornstarch. Fry the whole fish in hot coconut oil or ghee until it is cooked, then lift out and set aside. Chop the onions and fresh chillies. Grind the dry spices into a powder in an electric blender, adding the chopped ingredients and enough peanut oil to form a paste as the blades turn. Transfer to a wok and fry the paste until the spices are dark brown but not burned. (This needs careful watching as the oil can get hot enough to burn dry spices before an inattentive cook knows it.) Add the coconut milk, lime leaves, and salt to taste, and stir the mixture as it bubbles and thickens. Put in the fish and allow to cook without a lid until the oil separates from the rest of the sauce and the dish is fairly dry.

SAMBAL GORENG SETONG (Squid Sambal)

5 squid, cleaned, spines removed, and quartered
1 yellow onion, finely chopped and drained of moisture
4 Macadamia nuts or almonds
6 dried hot chillies
1 small stalk lemon grass, finely sliced
5 tablespoons tamarind water made from a piece of tamarind the size of a hazelnut (see p. 37)
1 tablespoon brown sugar
⅜ teaspoon blachan (shrimp paste)
paprika (optional)

First grind the nuts and chillies into a powder in an electric blender. Then put in the blachan and the onions and grind to a paste, adding oil to keep the blades turning.

Heat a little more oil in a wok or a frying pan and fry the spice paste and the lemon grass until it is dark brown and well cooked. Add the tamarind water and sugar, and stir. Turn down the heat a little, add the squid and cook it uncovered in the sauce until it looks oily, fairly dry and dark reddish-brown. As sambal goreng should be really dark red, which is hard to achieve without the small Bombay onions common in South East Asia, it may be necessary to add a teaspoon or so of paprika to achieve this effect.

SAMBAL GORENG IKAN BILIS
(Dried Whitebait Sambal)

3 oz. dried whitebait (from Chinese shops)
coconut oil or ghee
1 yellow onion, finely chopped and drained of all liquid possible

1 teaspoon lengkuas (laos) powder *or* 2 slices laos, chopped
1 stalk lemon grass, finely sliced
$\frac{3}{8}$ teaspoon blachan or shrimp paste
6 dried hot chillies
3 Macadamia nuts
$\frac{1}{2}$ cup tamarind water made from a small piece tamarind pulp
 (see p. 37)
$\frac{3}{4}$ cup thick coconut milk
salt
paprika (optional)

Pull the heads off the dried fish and wash. Leave the fish aside in a sieve for a while to dry out. Then deep-fry in plenty of hot coconut oil or ghee until crisp. Drain well, and keep them aside until the sauce is made.

In the meantime, grind the nuts and chillies into a powder in an electric blender. Then add the drained onions, lengkuas and blachan and blend to a paste, adding enough oil to keep the mixture moving in the machine. Transfer this oily paste to a wok or a frying pan over a high heat, add the lemon grass and allow the spices to fry until they are well cooked and dark brown. (They are cooked when they no longer adhere to the pan as you stir.) Now add the coconut milk, tamarind water and salt to taste, and let the sauce bubble uncovered until it is thick and dark red, with the oil floating on top. As with previous recipe it may be necessary to add a little paprika to achieve a sufficiently dark colour.

Finally, mix the fried whitebait and the sauce together and serve immediately for a deliciously crisp sambal.

GULAI AYAM (Chicken Curry)

1 chicken
2 medium yellow onions, grated, and the excess moisture squeezed
 out
1 stalk lemon grass, finely sliced
2 slices fresh laos (lengkuas), chopped *or* $\frac{1}{2}$ teaspoon dried
4 raw Macadamia nuts

⅜ teaspoon blachan or shrimp paste
4 tablespoons coriander seeds
1½ teaspoons cumin seeds
1½ teaspoons fennel seeds
1-inch-piece cinnamon bark
2 whole cloves
15 dried hot chillies
1½ teaspoons turmeric
⅜ cup vegetable oil
salt to taste
1 cup thick coconut milk
2 cups thin coconut milk

Chop the chicken into curry pieces (see p. 24). Put all the dry spices into a blender and grind finely. Heat the oil in a saucepan and when it is hot put in everything except the chicken and coconut milk. Fry the spices until they smell well cooked. Add a few spoonfuls of thick coconut milk, and stir the mixture so that you have a fairly thick sauce. Put in the chicken pieces and stir them around until they are well coated with the curry mixture. Add the thin coconut milk, stir again, cover the saucepan, and simmer until the chicken is tender. The curry must *not* dry up, so check occasionally as it cooks and add a little water if necessary. When it is almost ready add the rest of the thick coconut milk without stirring it in. Remove the pan from the fire and let it stand for a while before serving.

This curry can be prepared in the morning, left aside all day, and simply heated at dinner time.

CURRY KAPITAN

1 chicken (2 lbs.)
2 yellow onions
6 cloves garlic
10 fresh red chillies
½-inch-piece green ginger
½-inch-stick cinnamon bark
1½ teaspoons nutmeg

2 tablespoons coriander seeds
1 tablespoon cumin seeds
⅜ teaspoon mustard seeds
2 cardamom pods
½-inch-cube blachan, pounded
1 whole star anise
1½ teaspoons turmeric
salt to taste
⅜ cup coconut or peanut oil
3 cups thin coconut milk
¼ cup dried grated coconut
½ cup tamarind water made from a piece of tamarind pulp the
   size of a walnut (see p. 37)

For garnish

fried onion flakes
fresh chilli, cut in rounds

Cut the chicken into curry pieces (see p. 24). Grind all the dry spices to a powder in a blender and put this aside. Chop the onions, garlic, chillies and ginger. Brush a frying pan with oil and fry the dried coconut in this until it is light brown. Add this to the coconut milk and mix them thoroughly in a blender.

Heat the oil in a saucepan and fry the onions, garlic, ginger, chillies, blanchan and ground spices until they are brown and smell cooked. Put in the chicken pieces and stir. Add the coconut mixture and the tamarind water and simmer without a lid until the gravy is thick and the chicken tender (about 45 minutes). Serve in a large bowl, and garnish with dried onion flakes and rounds of fresh chilli.

AYAM KICHUP (Spiced Chicken)

This recipe comes from Che Hafsah Harun of Kuching, Sarawak. It is a dish for special occasions. It might be served, for instance, at the feast that precedes the fasting period. The recipe has been prepared in Che Hafsah Harun's family for three generations.

1 chicken (about 2½ lbs.)
4½ teaspoons laos (lengkuas) powder *or* 6 slices laos
2 stalks lemon grass
2-inch-piece green ginger, smashed and chopped
4 yellow onions, chopped and the excess moisture squeezed out
1 large clove garlic, peeled
20 dried chillies
2 cups tamarind water made from a piece of tamarind pulp the size
    of 2 walnuts (see p. 37)
¼ cup dark soya sauce
2 tablespoons sugar
⅜ cup vegetable oil
salt to taste

Cut the chicken into curry pieces (see p. 24). Heat the oil in a wok and fry the chicken pieces until they are brown. Drain and leave aside. In an electric blender, grind the laos, ginger, onions, garlic and chillies, adding oil to keep the mixture moving until it is a paste. Now transfer this oily paste to a wok or shallow pan and fry it over a high heat until the spices are brown and aromatic. Add the chicken pieces, and stir them as they fry for 2 minutes in order to coat them thoroughly with the spice mixture. Add the tamarind water, soya sauce, sugar, and lemon grass, bruised with a heavy knife-handle or a meat hammer. Allow to simmer without a lid until the chicken is tender, stirring occasionally. If the meat gets too dry before it is properly cooked, add more water and finish cooking. Adjust seasonings, and serve.

PANGGANG ITEK (Broiled Spiced Duck)

1 fresh duckling or chicken (about 2 lbs.)
    split and trussed Panggang style (see p. 24)
3 tablespoons coriander seeds
1 heaped tablespoon fennel seeds
1 tablespoon cumin seeds
1 teaspoon turmeric
¾ teaspoon nutmeg
¼ teaspoon mace

2-inch-piece cinnamon bark
4 cloves
3 cardamom pods
1½ teaspoons whole black pepper
½-inch-piece green ginger, smashed and chopped
1 stalk lemon grass, sliced fine
2 yellow onions, peeled and quartered
1 clove garlic
2 fresh chillies, sliced
tamarind water made from a piece of tamarind pulp the size of a
  hazelnut (see p. 37)
¾ cup thick coconut milk

Grind the dry spices to a powder in a blender. Stop the machine, put in all the other ingredients, except the meat, and grind to a thick paste. Coat the duckling freely with this paste.

Place the bird carefully on a broiling rack about 4 inches above a medium charcoal fire or wood-burning barbecue with low coals and no flame. Turn it occasionally and keep brushing on more of the spicy coconut milk paste as it cooks. This should take some time, and the cooked bird should be completely coated. Alternatively, the duck or chicken could be roasted in an oven using a dish with a rack or a rotisserie and frequently basted with the coconut milk mixture.

There is another version of Panggang Itek which leaves out the 'black' spices (nutmeg, mace, cinnamon, cloves, cardamom and pepper), using instead 1 tablespoon laos (lengkuas) powder and 3 Macadamia nuts. The procedure is otherwise the same as above.

GULAI DAGING LEMBU (Beef Curry)

1 lb. chuck steak
2 tablespoons coriander seeds
1 tablespoon fennel seeds
1 tablespoon cumin seeds
1-inch-piece cinnamon bark

135

6 cloves
2 points star anise
1½ teaspoons whole black pepper
1½ teaspoons turmeric
⅜ teaspoon nutmeg
5 dried hot chillies
1-inch-piece green ginger
2 cloves garlic
2 yellow onions
1 stem lemon grass, finely sliced
a piece of tamarind pulp mashed and softened in 1 tablespoon water
1 cup thick coconut milk
1 cup thin coconut milk
2 tablespoons coconut oil
2 tablespoons butter or ghee
salt to taste

Grind all the dry spices to a powder and mix with just enough water to form a thick paste. Cut the meat into cubes, mix together with the paste in a bowl and set aside until it is needed.

Chop the ginger, garlic and onions finely. Heat the coconut oil and butter or ghee, and when this is hot fry the ginger, garlic and onion mixture until well browned. Put in the spiced meat with the thin coconut milk and the lemon grass, cover, and let the pot simmer until the meat is tender. Turn the heat as low as possible, add the thick coconut milk and tamarind water, and reheat but do not boil. Add salt at the last minute.

MALAY SATAY

To most people Satay *is* Malay food. Tourists rarely pass through Malaya, or even Singapore, without making what amounts to a ritual visit to the street stalls that serve this delicacy.

In fact, Satay is only one of the many types of cooking embraced by the complex modern culture of the Malays and Indonesians. It is certainly one whose culinary reputation is very well deserved. But it could also be held up as the symbol of all the historical, cultural, and geographical influences that came together in this area in pre-colonial times: the kebab, reminiscent of the Arab Moslem world, the sauce a reminder of the Indianization which characterized the ancient period.

1 lb. fillet steak, round steak or chicken breast, cut into ½-inch cubes. Thread these on to a skewer about 6 inches long, leaving 3 inches at the holding end, and broil over a charcoal fire or under the broiler, basting occasionally with coconut or peanut oil.

Arrange the skewers of meat on a plate, pour over them the sauce described below and serve with cubes of fresh unpeeled cucumber. The Malays eat Satay with pieces of rice cake made from glutinous rice boiled and cooled under a press, which they dip in the sauce, but plain rice is just as acceptable.

Sauce

1 tablespoon coriander seeds
1½ teaspoons fennel seeds
1½ teaspoons cumin seeds
¾–1½ teaspoons ground chilli
1 teaspoon brown sugar
¼ cup tamarind water made from a piece of tamarind the size of a hazelnut (see p. 37)
¼-inch-cube blachan
2 yellow onions
1 clove garlic
¾ cup freshly roasted peanuts, roughly ground
¾ cup thick coconut milk
juice of ½ lemon
2 tablespoons peanut oil
salt to taste

Grind all the dry spices in a blender. Chop the onions and garlic finely and chop the blachan. Heat the oil in a saucepan and fry the onions and garlic, blachan and spices until they are well cooked and aromatic. Add the ground peanuts and coconut milk, tamarind water and sugar and stir well. Allow to simmer for 10 minutes and stir in the lemon juice just before serving.

MASAK LEMAK (Rich Vegetable Dish)

1 clove garlic
1 onion
3 oz. cooked shrimp, shelled and finely chopped
1 small cabbage or kale
a small piece of blachan, fried
1 cup thick coconut milk
1 cup thin coconut milk
2 or more fresh chillies (optional)

Chop or pound the onion, garlic, chillies and blachan into a paste. Finely shred the cabbage (or kale). Put the coconut milk and the spice paste into a saucepan, stir well, and bring to the boil. Finally add the cabbage and cook till tender. Add the shrimp just before the cabbage is cooked.

This dish is usually served with curried fish, but make sure that such a main course is followed only by fresh fruit as it will have been quite rich enough without a heavy pudding afterwards!

KACHANG BENDI GORENG RUMPAH
(Fried Spiced Green Vegetable) (Serves 4 or 10)

1 lb. green vegetable (okra, green beans or zucchini sliced in rounds)
½ lb. small raw shrimp, peeled and deveined
4 Macadamia nuts
5 dried chillies
2 yellow onions, finely chopped and the excess moisture squeezed out
1½ teaspoons blachan
5 tablespoons water
2–4 tablespoons peanut oil

Chop together all the spices, the nuts and the onions, then transfer them to a mortar and mash them into a fine paste. Heat the oil in a wok and fry the spice paste until it smells well cooked and no longer sticks to the pan. Then add the shrimp and stir-fry for a minute. Add the vegetables, and stir thoroughly. Add the water and salt to taste, and simmer uncovered until the vegetable is cooked but not soft.

'DYAK' AUBERGINE IN COCONUT MILK

This is a recipe from Sarawak. 'Dyak' aubergine is a local vegetable grown by farmers after they have burnt their fields prior to planting padi. It is the size of a grapefruit and is orange in colour when ripe. It is round and more sour in taste than other eggplant, but the dish is still good when made with the ordinary variety.

2 large eggplants
1½ yellow onions
4 small cloves garlic, peeled
1 stalk lemon grass, finely sliced
2 tablespoons dried shrimp
1½ level teaspoons blachan (shrimp paste), fried
6 dried chillies
2 cups thin coconut milk
salt to taste

Peel and dice the eggplant. Add the coconut milk and allow to simmer until the vegetable is nearly cooked. Meanwhile finely chop together the chillies, onions, garlic and shrimp paste; then pound them into a paste in a mortar. Add the dried shrimp and lemon grass, pounding them roughly in order to bruise but not break them, then mix well. Add this spice mixture to the half-cooked eggplant, add salt, stir, and simmer gently until the vegetable is done.

ACHAR AWAK (Mixed Pickled Salad) (Serves 12)

2 lbs. cucumber
½ lb. green beans

½ lb. eggplant
½ lb. carrot
½ lb. cabbage
3 yellow onions
20 fresh red chillies
6 cloves garlic
½-inch-cube blachan, roasted in foil (see p. 28)
1 lb. raw peanuts
2½ cups white vinegar
2 tablespoons sugar
1 tablespoon turmeric
salt to taste
2 cups peanut oil

Put the chillies, onions, garlic and blanchan through the fine blade of a grinder. Roast the peanuts in a pan on top of the stove until they are cooked, then when they are cool, roughly pound them. Cut all the vegetables into 2-inch by ½-inch strips. Do not peel the cucumbers. Lightly blanch each type of vegetable separately in boiling water.

Heat the oil in a wok. Fry the ground spices with the turmeric for 10 minutes, then add the vinegar, salt, sugar, and allow to boil. Add the peanuts and stir thoroughly. Put in the vegetables one kind at a time, and stir lightly to mix with the sauce.

TELOH DARDEH (Malayan Omelette)

1 yellow onion, chopped
2 fresh red chillies, sliced in rounds
chopped green part of 1 green onion
3 eggs beaten with 1 tablespoon water
salt to taste
a little peanut oil

Heat the oil until it smokes. Mix all the other ingredients, pour them into the pan and fry the omelette until it is cooked.

SAMBAL TUMIS (Fried Condiment)

3 dried chillies
1 small yellow onion, grated and the excess moisture squeezed out
1 tablespoon tamarind water made from a piece of tamarind pulp the
    size of a peanut (see p. 37)
1 tablespoon peeled and chopped raw shrimp
1 tablespoon brown sugar
salt to taste
peanut oil

Grind the dry chillies and mix together with onions, sugar and
salt. Heat a little oil in a pan, add the spices and fry until they
no longer stick to the sides. Add the tamarind water and let it
bubble, then throw in the shrimp and stir-fry until they are lightly
cooked. Serve as a tasty side dish with rice and other more
substantial dishes.

SAMBAL BLACHAN (Shrimp Paste Sambal)

This is the most common Malay side dish. It is very strong and
very potent, and not everyone will like it. In any case, only a
tiny quantity is placed on the edge of the plate, to be dipped into
cautiously.

8 fresh red chillies with their seeds
1-inch by 1-inch slice blachan, fried in foil (see p. 28)
2 lime leaves (optional)

Chop the leaves and the chillies finely. Transfer them to a mortar
with the blachan (stripped of its foil wrapper) and pound everything together into a paste. Serve in a small dish.

Chinese

ABALONE SOUP

1 can abalone, sliced
2 oz. Chinese mushrooms, soaked and sliced
$\frac{1}{4}$ stalk celery, chopped
3 green onions
5 slices green ginger, chopped
pork bones
$7\frac{1}{2}$ cups water
$\frac{1}{4}$ lb. lean ground pork
1 tablespoon salt
freshly ground black pepper to taste
$\frac{3}{4}$ teaspoon sugar
1 tablespoon dark soya sauce
$1\frac{1}{2}$ teaspoons cornstarch
1 tablespoon peanut oil
chopped green onions and watercress for garnish

Heat the oil in a saucepan and fry the ginger until brown. Add the pork bones and $7\frac{1}{2}$ cups water and simmer for $1\frac{1}{2}$ hours. When the stock is ready, remove the bones, add the celery, mushrooms and the meat which has been marinating in a mixture of soya sauce, cornstarch, salt, pepper and sugar. Allow to cook for 15 minutes.

Finally add the sliced and drained abalone, and allow it to heat through. Garnish the soup with chopped green onions and watercress, and serve in a large bowl.

FISH BALL SOUP

1 lb. Chinese fish balls (these can be bought fresh or canned from
   Chinese delicatessens)
2 small rolls *or* $\frac{1}{2}$ large roll Chinese vermicelli
2 pints fish or light chicken stock
salt, monosodium glutamate and light soya sauce to taste

For garnish

1 green onion, with leaves
1 whole sprig of very young celery (so young in fact that it has not
   really formed sticks yet, but consists largely of leaves on parsley-
   thin stalks) *or* 1 single stick of the more mature variety complete
   with leaves
1 fresh red chilli, seeds removed, sliced diagonally
lettuce shreds
fried onion flakes

Soak the vermicelli in cold water until it is soft. Bring the stock
to the boil and season with salt, monosodium glutamate and
light soya sauce to taste. Add the drained vermicelli and fish
balls and simmer until cooked. Pour the soup into a large bowl
and garnish with fried onion flakes, chopped spring onions and
celery, sliced chilli and shredded lettuce before serving.

Fish balls

If you cannot buy ready-made fish balls, it is possible to make
your own. It would be well worth the effort in any case, as the
store-bought variety are rather overloaded with flour.

1 lb. fine-fleshed whole fish (e.g. flounder, fluke, dab, sole, bluefish,
   hake)
¼ cup water
rice flour
salt to taste

Clean and scale the fish, and remove all flesh from the bones. The
heads and bones can then be used to make stock. Flake the fish
and pound it in a blender into a fine hash. Mix enough rice flour
to ½ cup of water to make a smooth stiff batter, adding salt.
Take a handful of the mixture and squeeze it out through a
clenched fist between thumb and forefinger in small balls. Use
these according to the preceding recipe.

CHICKEN SOUP

1 large chicken breast, boned and sliced across the grain
6 Chinese dried mushrooms
8-oz. can thinly sliced bamboo shoots
3 oz. very young whole snow peas (optional)
2 thin slices green ginger, chopped
1 clove garlic, crushed
4 cups thin chicken stock
1 tablespoon peanut oil
salt and pepper to taste
fried onion flakes (see p. 22) or chopped green leaves of green onion
    for garnish

Soak the mushrooms in hot water until they are soft. Drain and wash them, then remove the hard stalks and cut the mushrooms in half.

Heat the oil in a saucepan and fry the crushed garlic until it is brown. Add the chicken meat, stirring until it cooks, then add the stock, ginger and vegetables. Season to taste and allow all the ingredients to simmer together until the vegetables are cooked but still slightly crisp. Garnish the soup with fried onion flakes or, if you have not used snow peas, with chopped green leaves of green onion, and serve in a deep bowl.

Pork or shrimp soup may be made in the same way, substituting ½ lb. ground pork or shelled raw shrimp for the chicken and using coarsely chopped Chinese cabbage instead of the peas.

PORK SOUP

2 potatoes, peeled and diced
¼ lb. pork chop meat, boned and sliced across the grain
1 small roll *or* ¼ large roll of Chinese vermicelli
5 cups cold water
2 cloves
monosodium glutamate, pepper and salt to taste

Soak the Chinese vermicelli in cold water for 10 minutes until soft. Bring the 5 cups of water to the boil with the cloves. Add the potatoes and diced pork, and allow to simmer lightly until cooked. Add monosodium glutamate, salt and the drained vermicelli, and bring back to the boil. Sprinkle with a dash of freshly ground pepper and serve.

EGG-DROP SOUP

2 tablespoons peanut oil
1 clove garlic, chopped
¼ lb. chicken, beef or pork, thinly sliced
5 cups chicken stock or bouillon made from bouillon cubes
1 egg
2 green onions including the green part, finely sliced

Heat the oil in a saucepan and fry the garlic until it is brown. Add the meat and stir-fry until it changes colour. Then add the chicken stock, bring to the boil, cover and simmer for 5 minutes. Remove the pan from the fire and slowly and carefully stir in the egg, which should have been lightly beaten. The egg should not amalgamate with the soup, but should float in it in shreds. Finally add the green onions, stir and serve.

SHARKS' FIN SOUP

8-oz. package sharks' fins (obtainable from Chinese grocers), soaked in warm water for about 20 minutes, then drained (see below); you need about 2 cups after it is drained
⅜ lb. crab meat
3 oz. shredded chicken (optional)
the roe of 4 crabs *or* 2 eggs
1 egg (if using crab roe)
5 cups good chicken stock
1 tablespoon monosodium glutamate
1 tablespoon light soya sauce
1½ teaspoons salt
1 tablespoon sugar

1½ teaspoons sesame oil
a dash of pepper
5 tablespoons cornstarch
⅜ cup peanut oil or lard

In a big bowl, mash the crab's roe. Break in 1 egg and add ¼ cup water. Beat the mixture with chopsticks or a fork. If you are not using crab's roe, beat 2 eggs with ¼ cup water. Leave aside.

Combine the stock, monosodium glutamate, soya sauce, salt, sugar, sesame oil and pepper in a large bowl. Mix the cornstarch with ⅜ cup water for thickening the soup.

Heat the oil or lard in a pan and add the sharksfin. Pour in the stock mixture and a little extra water and boil for 30 minutes. Then drop in the chicken and crab. Slowly stir in the cornstarch and allow to thicken. Remove the pan from the fire, and while it is off the stove stir in the beaten egg and roe. Return to the fire and reheat, stirring all the time, but do not allow to boil.

Serve the soup in one large bowl from which guests help themselves.

To prepare sharks' fin

I have here used a package of sharks' fin which is already prepared, but in fact there are a number of forms in which one can obtain sharks' fin for Chinese cooking. It is merely a question of different preparations. Here are the various types and preliminary ways to handle them:

Packages of prepared sharks' fins. Soak in warm water for 20 minutes. Drain.

Dried large yellow sharks' fins. Boil for 1 hour, drain and shred.

Dried black sharks' fins. Boil for 2 hours, remove the black skin, and reboil for 1–2 hours in fresh water. Drain and shred.

(An 8-oz. package prepared sharks' fins = 16 oz. dried yellow sharks' fins = 1½–1¾ lbs. dried black sharks' fins.)

Raw sharks' fins. To prepare raw sharks' fins for use in soups or omelettes:

2 lbs. raw sharks' fins (including bones)
5 washed and cleaned green onions
2 small cloves peeled garlic
2 tablespoons peanut oil
1 tablespoon sherry
about 5 cups light chicken bouillon

Chop away the bone from the fins, then trim the fins' edge. Put them in a large saucepan in plenty of water and boil for 5 minutes. Remove the saucepan from the fire, cover, and leave the fins soaking in this way for about 4 hours.

After this time, remove the fins from the saucepan, wash in clean water and with a knife scrape away sand, skin and bones. Put the clean fins into a colander or bamboo sieve in another saucepan, place another colander or bamboo sieve over the fins with a plate or weight on top, then cover with plenty of fresh water. The 'cage' prevents the fins from coming loose while they are boiling. Place a lid on the saucepan, and let it simmer quietly for 6 or 7 hours, changing the water every 2 hours.

After this time drain the fins, pick off and discard the meat, wash the fins again and leave them in a colander to drain thoroughly. Heat the peanut oil in a pan and fry the whole spring onions and smashed garlic until light brown. Sprinkle in the sherry, then add chicken stock and simmer lightly for about 5 minutes. Remove onions and garlic. Put the cooked fins into the boiling liquor for 3 minutes, then drain once more. The fins are now ready for use.

FRIED SHARKS' FIN WITH SCRAMBLED EGG
(Serves 4)

4 oz. prepared sharks' fins (see preceding recipe) soaked in water for 20 minutes, then drained
¼ lb. boiled pork chop meat without bone, shredded
¼ lb. crab meat

4-oz. can bamboo shoots
4 eggs, lightly beaten
1 tablespoon chopped green ginger
5 tablespoons lard
1 tablespoon sesame oil
1 small yellow onion, chopped

Heat the lard and oil in a frying pan. Fry the ginger and onion until light brown. Add the pork, crab meat, bamboo shoots and sharks' fins, and stir–fry for about 10 minutes. Add the beaten eggs and stir well until the mixture is well amalgamated and dry.

SHRIMP IN BATTER

1 lb. raw jumbo shrimp
$\frac{1}{2}$ cup cornstarch
1 egg yolk
1 egg white
2 tablespoons water
salt and pepper
peanut oil for deep-frying

Shell and devein the shrimp, leaving on the tails. Wash and leave to drain. Sift the cornstarch, salt and pepper into a bowl. Make a well in the centre and put in the yolk and water. Beat slowly and lightly until smooth, and allow to stand for 15 minutes. Whisk the egg white until it is stiff and fold it into the flour mixture, making a thick batter.

Take each shrimp by the tail, dip it into the batter, and deep-fry in plenty of hot oil until golden brown.

SWEET AND SOUR WHOLE FISH

1 medium fish for steaming or frying (haddock, cod, sea bass, porgy, ocean perch, blackfish, etc.)
2 slices green ginger, finely chopped
2 whole slices green ginger (if fish is poached)
2 cloves garlic, smashed and chopped
a little plain flour

148

1 fresh red chilli
2 stalks onion
1 medium tomato
½ cucumber, unpeeled
1 lemon
1 tablespoon white vinegar
1 tablespoon light soya sauce
1 cup water
¼ cup sugar
1 tablespoon cornstarch
salt and pepper
peanut oil

Clean and scale the fish. Dry it. Make two or three slashes through to the bone across each side, rub the skin lightly with flour and leave aside. Squeeze the lemon and mix the juice with the water, vinegar, sugar, soya sauce, cornstarch, salt and pepper.

Fry the fish in a pan of hot oil until it is cooked. Alternatively, poach it by lowering it into water containing the two whole slices of green ginger as it comes to the boil. If the fish is to be cooked this way, however, it should not be coated with flour. Take off the heat, cover the pan and allow the fish to remain in the water for about 20 minutes, by which time it should be cooked through. When done, remove the fish from the pan but keep warm.

Put 1 or 2 tablespoons peanut oil in a pan and fry the chopped ginger and garlic until they are light brown. Add the sauce liquid, bring to the boil, and stir as it thickens. Pour over the fish immediately, and garnish with tomato wedges, green onions cut into 1-inch lengths, and thinly sliced chilli. Serve whole.

FRIED FISH WITH SOYA BEANS

1 fish for frying (about 1 lb.) (haddock, young cod, sole, flounder, fluke, porgy, sea bass, ocean perch, etc.)
peanut oil
2 slices green ginger, cut into strips
2 cloves garlic, sliced

2 oz. yellow soya beans (available at Chinese groceries in cans)
2 tablespoons water
a little sugar and soya sauce to taste
sliced fresh red chilli for garnish

Clean and scale the fish and dry it. Make two or three gashes
through to the bone on each side, and dust with flour.

Heat plenty of peanut oil in a wok and fry the fish until it is
cooked and crisp on the outside. Drain and set aside, keeping
the fish warm. Leaving 2 tablespoons oil in the pan, fry the garlic
and ginger until they are light brown. Mash the beans into a
paste, add this to the pan and stir-fry until it is brown and
cooked. Add 2 tablespoons water and the sugar and soya sauce,
stirring all together to produce a gravy. Pour this over the fish
and serve garnished with sliced fresh red chilli.

CHICKEN, BAMBOO SHOOTS AND MUSHROOMS

1 chicken (about 2 lbs.)
6–8 Chinese dried mushrooms, soaked and hard stalks removed
4-oz. can bamboo shoots, sliced
3 cloves garlic, crushed
1 tablespoon light soya sauce
$\frac{3}{4}$ teaspoon sugar
2 thin slices green ginger, cut into strips
flour
2 tablespoons peanut oil
$1\frac{1}{4}$ cups water
salt and pepper to taste

Chop the chicken into 3-inch pieces with bone and roll in flour.
Leave the mushrooms whole if small, halve them if large. Heat
the oil and fry the garlic and ginger until they are light brown.
Add the mushrooms and stir-fry for a few minutes. Add the
chicken and fry until well browned on all sides. Now add the
bamboo shoots and just enough water to cover the chicken (no
more then $1\frac{1}{4}$ cups and preferably less). Add the soya sauce, sugar
and seasonings, and cook until the chicken is tender. You can
mix in a little cornstarch if you want a thicker sauce.

CHICKEN IN THE NEST

This is a restaurant dish and therefore rather more trouble than many of the other recipes, but it is very decorative and worth the effort for a special dinner party. It comes from Mr. Tham Yui Kai of Lai Wah Restaurant in Singapore.

about ¾ lb. shredded chicken taken from a whole, fresh chicken
   weighing 1½ lb. when cleaned*
¾ oz. cooked ham, cut into fine strips
4-oz. can bamboo shoots, cut into rough strips
½–¾ yam or potato
1 tablespoon cornstarch
2 fresh red chillies
2 tomatoes
a few lettuce leaves
2 green onions
2 teaspoons medium-sweet sherry
3 Chinese dried mushrooms, soaked in water and hard stems
   removed (optional)
peanut oil for deep frying

Seasoning for chicken

¾ teaspoon monosodium glutamate
a dash of black pepper
½ of an egg white, unbeaten
1½ teaspoons salt
¾ teaspoon sugar
2 tablespoons water
2 tablespoons cornstarch

For the sauce

⅜ cup chicken stock
¾ teaspoon salt
¾ teaspoon sugar
1½ teaspoons sesame oil

*See p. 24 for instructions on how to bone a chicken in order to shred its meat tidily.

1 tablespoon cornstarch
¾ teaspoon monosodium glutamate
1 tablespoon light soya sauce
a dash of pepper

In a bowl, mix the chicken with its seasoning. When all is well blended, add 1 tablespoon peanut oil and mix again thoroughly. (The oil prevents the meat shreds from sticking together as they cook.) Leave aside for 15 minutes.

Cut the cleaned green onions into small pieces, wash and shred the lettuce. Remove the seeds from the red chillies, shred them and mix with the onions and lettuce for garnishing around the nest. Slice the tomatoes.

Peel the yam or large white potatoes, and cut into very fine, long matchsticks. (If you use potatoes, after cutting soak them in water to remove the starch and wash in a sieve until the water runs quite clear. Drain and thoroughly dry in a cloth, or better still, in the sun.) Mix with about 1 tablespoon of cornstarch and form them into a basket on a nest-shaped frying mould* (just like a ladle with holes). If you haven't such a mould, use a wire sieve with the handle bent perpendicularly to protect the cook's hand from hot fat. Place a smaller mould or sieve over the top of the potato nest and deep-fry in plenty of hot oil until the nest is crisp and stuck together. Drain and place on a serving plate surrounded by the shredded lettuce and tomato slices.

Mix together the ingredients for the sauce. Heat a clean pan or wok containing a lot of fresh oil. When it is hot put in the seasoned chicken shreds and deep-fry for about 30 seconds. Remove, drain and leave aside. Pour all but 2 tablespoons of oil out of the pan, throw in the bamboo shoots, green onions, Chinese mushrooms, which have been sliced, and the meat shreds, in that order, and stir–fry for a minute. Lastly, add the sherry and the sauce, mix thoroughly and allow to bubble and thicken. Spoon the mixture into the potato or yam nest, decorate the top with shredded ham and serve.

*These can sometimes be bought in Chinese shops.

FRIED OR ROAST CHICKEN

1 chicken (about 2 lbs.)
2 teaspoons honey
1 tablespoon boiling water
3 cloves garlic
1½ teaspoons dark soya sauce
peanut oil for deep frying

Cut the chicken into 6 large pieces. Mix all the other ingredients together and rub the chicken with the mixture. Leave aside until the pieces of chicken are quite dry. Deep-fry the chicken pieces in oil until they are golden brown. Drain and serve.

The chicken can also be roasted whole in the oven after rubbing with the mixture. If this method is followed, place the bird on a rack in an oven dish and baste frequently with the sauce as it cooks.

STEEPED CHICKEN

1 young, tender, *fresh* chicken
1½ teaspoons salt
1½ teaspoons pepper
3 slices green ginger
1 tablespoon dry sherry
watercress or Chinese parsley for garnish

For the sauce

1 tablespoon sesame oil
6 slices green ginger
salt and pepper

The chicken you use for this dish must be very fresh – preferably recently killed and plucked. Never attempt it with a defrosted bird.

Have ready a large pot of boiling water. Add salt, pepper, sherry and ginger. Put in the whole chicken and remove the

153

saucepan from the fire, allowing the chicken to steep for about 1 hour, by which time it should be lightly cooked though still faintly pink near the bone. This is the way the devotees prefer this dish, but if the thought does not appeal you can leave the chicken simmering in the pot for the first 15 minutes.

Remove the bird from the pot, drain it, and chop it into small pieces with the bone as described in Chapter 2, p. 24. An expert can put them all back together in the shape of the original chicken; but it takes a practised hand to bring this off successfully. Otherwise, arrange the pieces neatly.

Pour over it a sauce made from the six remaining slices of ginger, finely minced, lots of salt and pepper and the sesame oil. Garnish with watercress or Chinese parsley.

DRUNKEN CHICKEN

1 young tender chicken
5 tablespoons dark soya sauce
½ cup any Chinese wine or a pale, not too dry sherry
green onions unpeeled cucumbers, fresh red chillies, etc., for garnish

Lower the cleaned chicken into a saucepan of boiling water and simmer lightly for 30 minutes. Drain the cooked chicken and place it whole in a bowl. Pour over it a mixture of the soya sauce and wine, and leave it to marinate for several hours, spooning the juices all over the bird about every 30 minutes.

When it is well soaked, chop the whole bird into pieces the Chinese way (see p. 24), arrange them nicely on a dish, pour over the marinade and garnish on top as elaborately and decoratively as you like with the vegetables mentioned.

CHICKEN RICE DINNER

Serve a dish of Drunken Chicken (see above) with a bowl of boiled rice that has been cooked in the usual way, but using instead of plain water the stock in which the chicken was originally cooked plus a lump of pork fat. Have as a side dish for each person a mixture of the following:

8 medium cloves garlic, chopped
2 tablespoons green ginger, chopped
2 tablespoons fresh chilli, chopped and mixed well with salt,
    moistened with a little white vinegar

Heat any remaining stock from the chicken. Add a pinch of monosodium glutamate and some chopped green onions and serve as a soup after the chicken.

CHICKEN AND ALMONDS

1 large uncooked chicken breast, roughly shredded
2 small young carrots, diced
6 water chestnuts, diced
1 zucchini, diced
1 oz. bamboo shoots, sliced
4 Chinese dried mushrooms, soaked in warm water and the hard
    stems removed
3 cloves garlic, smashed and chopped
$\frac{1}{4}$ cup water
2 oz. blanched almonds
peanut oil

Split the blanched almonds and deep-fry in plenty of hot peanut oil until light brown. Drain and leave aside. Leaving about 2 tablespoons oil in the pan, lightly fry the water chestnuts. Remove, and leave aside. Slice and fry the mushrooms, and leave aside. Now fry the garlic until it is brown, add the chicken and stir-fry until the meat is cooked. Stir in all the other vegetables, including the water chestnuts and mushrooms, but not the almonds. Add about $\frac{1}{4}$ cup water, simmer uncovered for a minute, turn out onto a large plate, cover with the fried almonds, and serve.

CHICKEN ROLLS

1 lb. cooked chicken breasts, boned and cut into thin strips
¼ lb. pig's caul
½ oz. ham, cut into fine strips
½ oz. green ginger, cut into strips
3 stalks green onion, sliced
½ beaten egg
peanut oil for deep frying
cornstarch

Seasoning for chicken

¾ teaspoon salt
¾ teaspoon sugar
⅜ teaspoon monosodium glutamate
a dash of pepper
1 tablespoon Chinese oyster sauce
¾ teaspoon sherry
1 tablespoon cornstarch
1 tablespoon light soya sauce
1 tablespoon sesame oil

Mix the chicken and seasoning together well; then add 1 table-spoon peanut oil and mix again. Stand aside for at least 15 minutes.

Clean the pig's caul and wipe it dry. Cut into circular pieces about 6 inches in diameter (you should get about 10 pieces). Spread each piece of caul flat and put in its centre some chicken, ham, ginger and green onion. Fold in the sides and roll up like a sausage. Seal with beaten egg and roll lightly in cornstarch.

Deep-fry the rolls for 1 minute in plenty of very hot peanut oil which has been removed from the heat. Replace on the stove and fry for further 3 minutes. Drain and serve.

FRIED CHICKEN WRAPPED IN PAPER

1 chicken (2½–3½ lbs.)

Seasoning for chicken

¾ teaspoon salt
1 tablespoon sugar
1½ teaspoons Ve-tsin or monosodium glutamate
1½ teaspoons sesame oil
1 tablespoon light soya sauce
1 tablespoon ginger juice (see p. 33)
1 tablespoon sherry
2 tablespoons Chinese oyster sauce
2 tablespoons vegetable oil
1 tablespoon cornstarch
a dash of black or white pepper
vegetable oil for deep frying

Cut the chicken into pieces normally used in curry dishes (see p. 24). Mix all the seasonings together and marinate the chicken in this mixture for at least 2 hours, preferably more. After this has been done, wrap each piece of chicken in a square of grease-proof paper, folding it as indicated in the figure on p. 158. Tuck in the corner at no. 5 to prevent the package from falling apart. Deep-fry in plenty of hot oil until the paper is light brown. Lift out, remove the paper, arrange the chicken pieces on a plate and serve.

SLICED CHICKEN IN PAPER

1 lb. chicken breast, boned and thinly sliced across the grain
½ package frozen peas
8 Chinese dried mushrooms, soaked and hard stems removed
1 tablespoon sesame oil
1 tablespoon medium sweet sherry
½-inch-piece green ginger, cut in strips
2 tablespoons Chinese oyster sauce
a dash of pepper
oil for deep frying

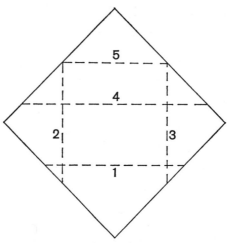

Season the meat with the oyster sauce, sesame oil, pepper and sherry, then mix it with the ginger strips. Cut greaseproof paper into 6-inch squares, put a heaping teaspoon of peas, 1 of meat and 2 or 3 slices of mushroom on to each square, and wrap it up as in the above figure. Fry the packets in deep hot oil for 10–15 minutes, turning occasionally. Serve the chicken in its paper packets.

ROAST CRISPY CHICKEN

1 fresh (not frozen) chicken (about 2 lbs.)
1 tablespoon 'Five Spices Powder' (available in Chinese groceries)
1 tablespoon chopped fresh red chilli
1 tablespoon freshly ground cinnamon bark
2 points star anise
1 sprig parsley
$\frac{1}{2}$ lemon
3 stalks green onion, sliced
1 tablespoon strong honey or corn syrup
plenty of oil for deep frying

Wash the chicken inside and out and dry it. Rub all over with 1 tablespoon 'Five Spices Powder' mixed with 1 tablespoon salt.

Simmer the chilli, star anise, and cinnamon bark in just under 4 cups water for 5 minutes. Lift out the chilli and cinnamon and stuff them with the green onions and parsley inside the chicken. Holding the bird over the pan, ladle the boiling spiced water over it several times. Allow to dry.

In the meantime mix the honey or corn syrup with 2 cups water and the half lemon cut in two. Bring this mixture to the boil and thoroughly coat the chicken with it. Now tie a string round the chicken's neck and hang the bird in a warm, dry place, preferably in the sun, for 3 or 4 hours to drain and dry thoroughly. (This lengthy process can be shortened and the bird protected from flies if you are lucky enough to own an electric hair dryer of the hand-held type. Using this machine you would achieve the necessary dryness in about 20 minutes.) It can then be roasted in an oven in the normal way, or deep-fried whole in plenty of hot oil for 15–20 minutes.

Cut the cooked chicken into serving pieces and serve with individual small dishes of spiced salt made from table salt and 'Five Spices Powder' in the proportion of 6:1.

CHICKEN IN HOT SAUCE (Straits Chinese)

1 boiling hen (about 2 lbs.), cut into curry pieces (see p. 24)
2 large yellow onions, chopped
3 red chillies, sliced in rounds without removing seeds
$\frac{3}{8}$ cup vegetable oil (peanut or coconut)
$\frac{1}{4}$ cup thick soya sauce
3 tablespoons white vinegar
2 teaspoons brown sugar
$1\frac{1}{4}$–2 cups water
salt to taste

Heat the oil in a shallow frying pan or a wok, add the chopped onions and fry until they are soft. Add the sliced chillies and the chicken pieces and brown. Pour in the rest of the ingredients, bring to the boil and simmer until the chicken is tender and there is a good brown sauce. Keep the pan covered until the meat is nearly cooked. Then remove the lid, reducing the sauce a little as the chicken finishes cooking.

PEKING DUCK

1 fat fresh duck (about 2–3 lbs. when cleaned; never use a soggy
  frozen duck for this princely dish)
¾ teaspoon Chinese 'Five Spices Powder' (available in Chinese
  groceries)
1 tablespoon salt
2–4 tablespoons Chinese oyster sauce
¼ lb. fresh bean sprouts
peanut oil for deep frying

For the soup

green onion tops, chopped
a few leaves of young spinach or Chinese cabbage
monosodium glutamate

For side-dishes

thin slices fresh white bread
strips of young cucumber, unpeeled
whole green onions

Syrup mixture

2 tablespoons honey or corn syrup ⎫
½ cup water   ⎪ Boil all the ingredients together
1 tablespoon white vinegar   ⎬ until well blended
1½ teaspoons light dry sherry   ⎭

Wash the duck and dry it with paper towels. Combine the 'Five Spices Powder' and salt, and rub the inside of the duck well with this mixture. Now comes an essential part of the whole cooking process if you are going to achieve the correct, sought-after crispness of the skin, which is enjoyed as a separate course. *Pour boiling water over the duck, held in a colander, at least 6*

160

times, allowing the bird to dry thoroughly between each immersion. Brush it well all over with the syrup mixture described above and hang it on a string in a warm dry place, preferably in the sun, for a few hours until it is quite dry, or use an electric hair dryer as suggested above in the recipe for Roast Crispy Chicken. When it is dry, deep-fry the whole duck in plenty of hot oil for about 30 minutes.

Peking Duck is served as three separate courses. First make the plum sauce described below. Then carve off the entire crisp skin in pieces. Serve the skin on a plate with side-dishes of the plum sauce, thin slices of fresh white bread, which has been pre-heated in the oven and the crusts removed, whole green onions and strips of young cucumber complete with skin. Each diner places pieces of duck skin, onion and cucumber on a slice of bread, tops them with plum sauce, folds the whole over in rough sandwich style, and eats.

Plum sauce
dark plum jam
white vinegar

Mix together enough of the jam and white vinegar in the proportions 4 teaspoons jam: 3 teaspoons vinegar to provide a small dish full of the sauce.

Second, cut the duck meat off the carcass in strips, season with the oyster sauce, and stir-fry in a little oil with the bean sprouts. Serve this with two or three other dishes and plain boiled rice.

Finally, chop up the carcass, cover it with water, add a pinch of monosodium glutamate, and bring to the boil. Add some chopped green onion tops and green leafy vegetable such as very young spinach, or Chinese cabbage, and serve the resulting soup last in a large bowl.

SEASONED SHREDDED PORK (Serves 2 or 4)

½ lb. pork chop meat or pork loin, bone removed and the meat
  sliced
cornstarch
peanut oil
2 cloves garlic, crushed
1 tablespoon dark ṣoya sauce
1½ or 3 teaspoons sugar, according to taste
a dash of freshly ground pepper
lard

Roll the meat very lightly in cornstarch, add a little peanut oil to
moisten. Mix it with garlic, soya sauce, sugar and pepper in a
bowl. Heat the lard, throw in the seasoned meat, and stir-fry
until it is cooked, adding a dash of water to moisten.

This dish can be made with onion rings instead of garlic for a
change. Slice one large yellow onion, fry the slices lightly in the
hot lard first, then add the meat which has been seasoned with
everything but garlic, and stir-fry as above.

SWEET AND SOUR PORK

1½ lbs. pork meat, half lean, half fat (loin is best, but sowbelly will
  do if it is skinned)
1 tablespoon light soya sauce
salt and pepper to taste
sprigs of parsley and fresh red chillies for garnish

For the batter

9 heaping tablespoons wheat flour
11–12 tablespoons water
about 4 drops dark soya sauce
salt and pepper to taste

Cut the meat into 1-inch cubes, season it with the light soya
sauce, salt and pepper and put aside. Mix all the ingredients for
the batter together in a bowl. (This must be thick enough to
coat the meat.)

Heat plenty of peanut oil to boiling point for deep frying. Coat the seasoned pieces of meat with the batter and drop them one by one into the boiling oil. Turn the heat down to medium and fry the meat pieces until they are dark brown. This will take about 20 minutes. In the meantime in another pan prepare the sweet and sour sauce as described below. Add the drained pieces of fried pork to the sauce, mix well and serve, garnishing the dish with sprigs of parsley and fresh red chillies, cut in rounds or soaked into flower shapes (see p. 23).

Sweet and sour sauce

2 tablespoons white vinegar
1 tablespoon light soya sauce
1½ cups water
7 tablespoons sugar
4½ teaspoons cornstarch
salt and pepper to taste
a few slices parboiled carrot, green pepper and pineapple (optional)
   or 1 small can Chinese pickled vegetables

Mix all these ingredients in a bowl and put aside. While the pork is frying heat the mixture in a pan, stirring well until it boils. Add the pickled vegetables last if you are using them.

OVEN BARBECUED PORK

a piece of pork loin *or* sowbelly of any weight

Marinade

For each pound of meat use:
¾ teaspoon 'Five Spices Powder'
2 tablespoons dark soya sauce
2 tablespoons hot water
1 tablespoon honey
1 tablespoon sugar
⅜ teaspoon roughly ground black pepper
3 cloves garlic, crushed
salt to taste

Whichever piece of meat you use, turn it skin-side down and cut between the bones as far as necessary to separate them but without reaching through the fat to the skin.

Place the marinade mixture in a dish large enough to hold the meat, and allow the pork to marinate in this for 2–4 hours, turning it about occasionally.

Lift out the meat. Pour boiling water over the skin and allow it to dry. In the meantime heat the oven to 400° F. Place the meat on a rack in a roasting dish with its skin uppermost (or best of all, if you have one, spear it on a rotisserie). Allow to cook for about 1 hour or until done. You will have to keep your eye on the oven throughout the cooking as the meat may burn.

PORK SAMBAL (Straits Chinese?)

This is probably a Straits Chinese dish, using a toned-down Malay sambal method to cook pork which would not be eaten by Moslem Malays but by Chinese. The use of the Indian ghee, however, marks it as somewhat intercommunal.

1 lb. pork chop meat, boned and cut into thin slices
3 yellow onions
3 or 4 small cloves garlic
6 dried chillies
1 tablespoon fennel seeds
2-inch-stick cinnamon
juice of ½ lemon
salt to taste
2 tablespoons ghee
2 tablespoons coconut oil

Chop the onion and garlic finely, squeeze out and discard all excess water. Grind fennel seeds and chillies to a powder in a blender. Heat the ghee and the coconut oil in a wok or a heavy saucepan, and fry onion mixture and spice powder until they are dark brown. Add the meat, the whole cinnamon stick, salt to taste and a dash of water, stir, and let it simmer, uncovered, for about 15 minutes. Remove from the fire, stir in the lemon juice, and it is ready to serve.

PORK SATAY (Straits Chinese)

1 lb. pork chop meat cut away from the bone *or* boneless pork loin
3 large yellow onions
8 fresh hot red chillies
1½ teaspoons blachan or shrimp paste
2 stalks lemon grass
6 Macadamia nuts
1 tablespoon coriander seeds
1½ teaspoons salt
1 tablespoon sugar
1 cup thick coconut milk
5 tablespoons peanut oil
cucumber slices for garnish

Put the onions and chillies through the fine blade of a grinder, and then mash them further in a mortar. Wrap the blachan in an envelope of foil and roast it in a frying pan on top of the stove for a few minutes until it smells cooked. Remove from its wrapper and pound with the onion mixture. Grind the Macadamia nuts, coriander, salt and sugar in an electric blender, add the coconut milk and oil, then the onion mixture, and mix them all together into a sauce in the machine. Pour into a shallow bowl, and stir in the lemon grass which has been finely sliced.

Cut the pork into cubes about ½-inch by ½-inch by ½-inch and marinate the cubes of meat in the sauce for at least 1 hour. Thread the meat on small skewers or bamboo broiling sticks (leaving 2 or 3 inches clear on the handle end for holding the sticks). Broil over a charcoal fire or under the broiler, dipping the meat-laden skewers occasionally into the sauce as they cook. Serve with plain rice and cucumber slices.

KIDNEY FLOWER

½ cauliflower
1 pork kidney
⅜ lb. raw shrimp
3 cloves garlic
light soya sauce
1-inch-piece green ginger, chopped and moistened if necessary
a pinch of sugar

Cut up the cauliflower into flowerets and parboil until *very* lightly cooked. Clean the kidney well, removing all the tubes, and cut it into cubes with a floral design. (To achieve this, first cut the whole kidney into halves lengthwise, and remove the central core of tubes. Then take each half and place it on a cutting board with the outside up. With a sharp knife cut crisscross diagonal lines *half way through* each half kidney, and then cut the kidneys through and across into 1-inch cubes.) Season the meat with pepper, salt, sugar, 2 teaspoons light soya sauce and the squeezed juice from the ginger.

Shell and devein the shrimp and season them with a little sugar.* Mix them in with the seasoned kidneys. Heat 1 tablespoon of peanut oil in a pan. Flatten the garlic cloves with a knife, and fry them in the oil until they are brown and have imparted their aroma, then remove and discard them. Now put the shrimp and kidneys into the pan and fry lightly. Add the cauliflower and stir-fry. Lastly, add 2 teaspoons light soya sauce and a little water if necessary, and stir until everything is well mixed and heated through.

GINGER BEEF

1¼ lbs. rump steak, thinly sliced across the grain
¼ lb. green ginger, sliced into very fine shreds

* Always season raw shrimp with sugar rather than salt. This ensures that the flesh remains firm and white as it cooks.

¾ lb. sliced bamboo shoots (optional)
1½ teaspoons sesame oil
2 tablespoons dark soya sauce
1½ teaspoons cornstarch
sugar to taste
peanut oil

Mix the meat with soya sauce, cornstarch and sugar in a bowl. Stand aside to season.

Heat a little oil in a pan, throw in the ginger, and fry until it is brown and crisp. Add the seasoned meat and bamboo shoots and stir-fry until it is cooked. After removing the pan from the fire, just before serving, stir in 1½ teaspoons sesame oil. Serve with plain rice and other dishes.

SHREDDED BEEF AND VEGETABLES
(Serves 3 without any other dishes)

½ lb. rump steak
4 oz. cauliflower, broken into small flowerets
1 green pepper, thickly sliced
3 oz. bamboo shoots, sliced
4 oz. carrots, cut into matchstick lengths
10 Chinese dried mushrooms, soaked in warm water and the hard
  stems removed
4 cloves garlic, chopped
4 thin slices green ginger
1 cup water
1½ teaspoons cornstarch
1½ teaspoons sugar
1½ teaspoons dark soya sauce
peanut oil
pepper and salt

Shred the steak thinly, mix it with the cornstarch, ¾ teaspoon of the sugar, and soya sauce, and leave aside. Heat 4 tablespoons peanut oil and fry half of the garlic until golden. Add the cauliflower, green pepper and carrots, and stir-fry until they are lightly cooked but still crisp, then add the bamboo shoots and mushrooms, which have been diced, and stir-fry a moment longer. Remove the vegetables and set aside.

Heat a little more oil and fry the remaining garlic and ginger. Add the meat and fry until it is just cooked. Now mix together the water, pepper, salt, the remaining $\frac{3}{4}$ teaspoon sugar and a little more soya sauce. Add this to the meat in the pan and stir. Add the vegetables, let the dish bubble once, and serve immediately.

ZUCCHINI, EGG AND SHRIMP

$\frac{3}{4}$ lb. zucchini, cut into matchstick lengths
$\frac{1}{2}$ lb. peeled and deveined raw shrimp
2 cloves garlic, chopped
2 tablespoons peanut oil
1 egg
salt to taste

Heat the oil and stir-fry the garlic, then the shrimp and then the zucchini. Cover the pan and cook until tender but not soft. Remove the lid, add salt to taste, break in the egg, and stir vigorously until all the ingredients are well mixed and the egg is cooked.

Shredded cabbage is also good cooked this way.

STIR-FRIED BEANS

1 lb. green beans, cut into 1-inch lengths
$\frac{1}{2}$ lb. pork chop meat, finely sliced
2 cloves garlic, chopped
salt to taste
2 tablespoons peanut oil
monosodium glutamate (optional)

Heat the oil until it smokes. Brown the garlic in the oil, then add the pork, stirring until it has lost its raw look. Last add the beans, salt, and a pinch of monosodium glutamate, and stir until the vegetable is lightly cooked but not soft. Add a dash of water and cover the pan if you prefer a slightly moister dish, but this is not really necessary.

Almost any vegetable can be cooked this way – bean sprouts, Chinese cabbage, spinach, peas or rounds of zucchini, to name only a few – and you can use peeled and deveined raw shrimp instead of pork.

MALAYAN CABBAGE

1 small cabbage, finely shredded
¼ lb. finely chopped pork (use the meat from a loin chop)
a few raw shrimp, peeled and deveined (optional)
1 medium yellow onion, finely chopped or grated
1 or more fresh hot chillies according to taste, finely sliced, seeds
  removed
1 tablespoon peanut oil

Heat the oil in a frying pan. Fry the shrimp, pork, drained onion, and chilli until they are cooked. Add the cabbage and salt to taste. Stir-fry until the cabbage is wilted but is not soft. It should still be slightly crisp when eaten.

STIRRED TOMATOES OR SILVER BEET
WITH BLACK BEANS

2 teaspoons Chinese black beans (available at Chinese groceries)
1 lb. tomatoes, roughly chopped
1 tablespoon peanut oil
chopped green onions for garnish

Wash the black beans, and drain. Heat the oil in a frying pan, add the beans and fry a little. Add the chopped tomatoes and stir-fry until cooked but not too soft. Dish onto a plate and garnish with chopped green onions.

169

This dish is also good using sliced silver beet instead of tomatoes. It goes well with Ginger Beef (see p. 166).

STUFFED BITTER CHINESE CABBAGE
(KAI CHOY)

Bitter Chinese cabbage is also known as mustard greens. It is not to be confused with sweet Chinese cabbage (Bak Choy), which is too soft for this dish. Large stalks of celery or chicory could perhaps be substituted.

1 lb. Kai Choy
1 tablespoon pork fat or chicken fat
1 bamboo shoot
½ lb. raw shrimp, unpeeled
⅜ lb. fresh crab meat *or* 6-oz. can
½ egg, beaten
a little cornstarch
1¼ cups chicken stock

Seasoning for shrimp paste

¾ teaspoon salt
⅜ teaspoon monosodium glutamate
⅜ teaspoon sugar
a dash of pepper

For the sauce

¾ teaspoon monosodium glutamate
¾ teaspoon sesame oil
1½ teaspoons salt
¾ teaspoon sugar
a dash of pepper
4 teaspoons cornstarch mixed with 1 tablespoon water

Clean and shell the shrimp, then dry them. Finely chop the pork fat, the shrimp and the bamboo shoot *separately*. Squeeze dry the bamboo shoot after chopping. If you are using uncooked crab meat, steam it and flake the flesh.

Cut away the leaves from the vegetables, leaving only those

170

parts of the stalks that are suitable for stuffing. Cook them, uncovered, in boiling water for 5 minutes or until just soft. Drain, and leave them to soak in cold water. When cool, drain again, and cut into 3-inch lengths.

Mix together the ingredients for the seasoning for shrimp paste. Mix the chopped shrimp with the pork fat and shrimp seasonings and knead into a fine paste with your hands. After this has been done, stir the chopped bamboo shoot into the paste. Sprinkle the vegetables with a little cornstarch to make them dry, and stuff each length with shrimp paste. In a little hot oil in a pan, fry them on the side of the shrimp paste until it is cooked, then lift them out and drain off the excess oil carefully. Keep warm.

Boil the stock until it reduces by half. Add this bit by bit to the sauce ingredients in another pan, stirring all the time, until the sauce comes to the boil and thickens. Stir in the crab meat and, when it returns to the boil, remove from the fire and stir in the beaten egg. Replace the saucepan on the fire, stirring again until it reaches boiling point. Now pour the sauce over the stuffed vegetable, and serve.

JAR GAR NAN (Straits Chinese) (Serves 10)

1 lb. freshly roasted peanuts
2–4 teaspoons ground chilli
1¼ cup tamarind water made from ½ cup tamarind pulp (see p. 37)
1 tablespoon salt
2 tablespoons sugar
½-inch-piece of blachan, fried and pounded
¼ lb. green beans, cut into 2-inch lengths and boiled lightly
10 hard-boiled eggs, shelled and halved
1 lb. very young spinach, cut into 1-inch pieces and blanched lightly,
  or an equivalent amount of watercress, *or* 1 lb. lotus stem, sliced*

* Lotus stem can sometimes be bought fresh in Chinese delicatessens, and is also available already cooked in cans or dried in packages. If you can manage to get hold of a fresh one, peel it, slice it in rounds, and blanch the rounds in boiling water.

Lotus stem is a very attractive vegetable for this dish. When prepared it looks rather like a transverse section of the bullet-chamber of a six-shooter.

½ lb. cabbage, finely shredded and blanched lightly
6 cubes fresh bean curd, cut into ½-inch cubes and deep fried until
   crisp and brown
½ lb. potatoes, peeled, boiled and sliced

Pound nuts roughly. Put the ground chilli, pounded blachan, salt and sugar into a large bowl. Add the strained tamarind water slowly and mix, then add the nuts and mix thoroughly. Adjust the thickness of this sauce to a suitable consistency, adding water if necessary. Arrange the vegetables, eggs and bean curd in separate heaps on a large platter, and pour the sauce over.

STUFFED SQUASH OR ZUCCHINI RINGS

2 small zucchini *or* 1 whole squash
¾ lb. finely chopped pork loin or finely chopped raw shrimp
1 yellow onion, finely chopped
2 cloves garlic, crushed
1½ teaspoons light soya sauce
1 tablespoon cornstarch
lard or peanut oil
chopped green onions for garnish

Peel the zucchini, cut it into thick rings, and scoop out the seeds If you use squash, peel them and remove the seeds, but otherwise leave whole. Steam the vegetable until it is just soft. Drain, and leave aside.

Mix meat or shrimp, soya sauce, and cornstarch together. Lightly fry the garlic and onion in hot oil, add the meat mixture, and stir-fry everything together thoroughly until the meat or shrimp changes colour.

Use the mixture to stuff the squash or zucchini rings. Heat oil in a pan and fry the stuffed vegetable, meat-side down, until the meat is cooked. Turn once, taking care not to dislodge any stuffing, if you have used zucchini rings. Serve immediately, sprinkling chopped green onion over the top of the dish.

This dish is also delicious steamed. Cut the zucchini in half

lengthwise instead of into rings, stuff it, put the two halves together again and steam in a plate sitting on a rack over boiling
water in a covered saucepan.

CHAP-CHYE (Serves 3 as a single dish)

1 oz. Chinese vermicelli, soaked for 20 minutes in cold water
1 tablespoon cloud ear or tree fungus (available at Chinese groceries)
⅛ large cabbage, roughly cut, *or* 4 large sticks celery
1 oz. Chinese dried mushrooms, soaked in warm water and the hard
    stems removed
about 60 (roughly 1 oz.) dried lily buds (available at Chinese
    groceries)
4-oz. can bamboo shoots, sliced
5 tablespoons water from the can of bamboo shoots
1 oz. dried bean curd sheet, soaked in warm water for 15 minutes.
    (You can use instead 1 oz. dried bean curd twists. These are in
    many ways more interesting to eat, but because they are much more
    solid, they must be soaked overnight, and take longer to cook)
6 slices green ginger, chopped
3 green onions with green tops
¾ teaspoon monosodium glutamate
1 tablespoon dark soya sauce
¾ teaspoon cornstarch
1½ teaspoons Chinese wine or sherry
salt to taste
a dash of pepper
5 tablespoons peanut oil
1½ teaspoons sesame oil

If you have the patience, tie a knot in the middle of each lily bud.
This will stop the vegetable from breaking up as it cooks, and
will keep the texture as it should be. Cut the soaked bean curd
into 1-inch by 1½-inch pieces. Heat the peanut oil in a wok or a
large frying pan. Add the ginger and brown it. If you have used
twisted bean curd add it now and stir-fry a little. Throw in the
cabbage, sliced mushrooms, and cloud ear or tree fungus, in that
order, and stir-fry. Add the bamboo shoot water, lily buds,
bamboo shoots and the cornstarch which has been mixed with the

soya sauce, sherry, salt and pepper, and stir until everything is lightly cooked (the cabbage or celery should be done but still crisp).

If you are using bean-curd sheet, add this last with the vermicelli as these both tend to stick to the pan. Just before lifting off the fire, sprinkle with the cleaned green onions sliced into small pieces and the monosodium glutamate. After taking the pan off the stove, stir in the sesame oil, and serve.

For a vegetarian lunch, serve chap-chye with plain rice. If you would like it to be a little more substantial, you can put a 'coin-purse' egg on top of each portion, or some cubes of the bean curd cheese that you buy in cans in Chinese shops. (To make 'coin-purse' eggs, break a whole egg into a little hot peanut oil in a frying pan and fry *on both sides* to the degree desired.)

To make chap-chye with meat, add slices of pork, beef or pork liver after frying the ginger. Stir-fry until the meat changes colour, then proceed as above. In this case, don't put anything extra on top of the cooked dish.

FRIED RICE

3 cups cold, cooked rice
2 eggs, beaten with salt to taste
½ lb. peeled, cooked shrimp
¼ lb. Sar Chiew (Chinese roast pork) or thick slab bacon, cubed
¼ lb. Chinese sausages (optional)
1 yellow onion, chopped
1 green onion, especially the green part, chopped
seasoned water made from 5 tablespoons water, 1½ teaspoons salt,
    1½ teaspoons monosodium glutamate (Ve-tsin) and 3 tablespoons
    light soya sauce
peanut oil

Heat 2 teaspoons oil in a pan and fry the beaten eggs, stirring them into separate pieces as they cook. In another pan, heat some more oil and fry the chopped brown onion, adding the shrimp and a dash of light soya sauce. Remove this mixture from the pan and set it aside. Fry the sausages, lift them out and cut them up. Fry the Sar Chiew, or bacon in the latter case adding a dash of light soya sauce, and remove.

Now fry the rice, stirring in more oil as you go until each grain is well coated. Still stirring, sprinkle the seasoned water over it, then add the Sar Chiew or bacon, the shrimp, sausages, eggs and lastly the green onions, continuing to stir all the time.

These quantities are intended when fried rice is to be served *on its own* as a supper or luncheon dish. If it is to be only a side dish, don't use as much meat as is suggested here. Use *either* Sar Chiew *or* Chinese sausages, but not both.

FRIED BEE-HOON

½ lb. Chinese vermicelli (Bee-Hoon)
½ lb. small green prawns or raw shrimp
½ lb. bean sprouts, with the heads pulled off
2 yellow onions, sliced
1 bunch mustard leaves or watercress
1 abalone, canned (or already pressure-cooked if fresh)
10 cloves garlic, crushed

For garnish

2 tablespoons soya sauce
1 cup water
pepper, salt, sugar and extra soya sauce to taste
peanut oil
2 eggs
1 unpeeled cucumber, sliced into rounds
2 chillies, cut into strips
fried onion slices
celery leaves

Soak the Chinese vermicelli in cold water for 10 minutes, drain and leave aside. Shell and devein the prawns or shrimp. Tear the mustard leaves into 2-inch lengths and slice the abalone into thin strips.

Beat the eggs and fry them as a thin pancake. Slice the pancake into fine strips and use as a garnish later. Heat a little peanut oil in a wok or a frying pan, and fry the onions until they are brown. Drain and keep aside.

Add a little more oil to the pan, fry the garlic, and when it is light brown stir in, one at a time, the prawns, abalone, bean sprouts and lastly the mustard leaves. Add the water mixed with the seasonings. Let it bubble, then dish this mixture on a plate and leave aside. Add a little more oil and fry the vermicelli for a few minutes. Stir in the cooked ingredients until everything is hot. Now serve on a plate and scatter the egg strips, cucumber, chillies, fried onion slices and celery leaves, over the top.

FRIED EGG NOODLES

$\frac{3}{4}$ lb. Chinese egg noodles
1 lb. lean pork or chicken, chopped
6 Chinese dried mushrooms, soaked and the hard stems removed
$\frac{1}{2}$ lb. young green beans, chopped (optional)
3–4 stalks celery
1 small can bamboo shoots, cut into fine strips
2 cloves garlic, smashed and chopped
3 slices green ginger, chopped
$1\frac{1}{2}$ teaspoons sherry
1 tablespoon dark soya sauce
$1\frac{1}{2}$ teaspoons cornstarch
9 tablespoons peanut oil

For garnish

2 eggs
green onions

Put the noodles in salted boiling water for 5 minutes and untangle them. Drain and leave aside. Mix the meat with sherry, soya sauce and cornstarch and set aside.

Heat 1 tablespoon oil in a pan and make a thin omelette with the 2 lightly beaten eggs. Slice it up into fine strips and leave aside.

Heat 3 tablespoons oil in the pan and stir-fry the seasoned meat. Dish up and leave aside.

In a clean pan heat 1 tablespoon oil. Fry the ginger and garlic until brown, slice the mushrooms and add them with all the remaining ingredients; stir-fry until cooked. Dish up and leave aside.

Heat 4 more tablespoons oil in a wok or large pan. Add the noodles and stir until they are heated through. Add meat and vegetables and mix thoroughly until everything is hot. Serve on a large plate, and garnish with chopped spring onions and omelette strips.

SPRING ROLLS I. (Straits Chinese)
(Makes 12–15 rolls)

It is often possible to buy ready-made spring roll (egg roll) skins in Chinese delicatessens or noodle factories. If you can, by all means do so, as it will save a lot of trouble and may prove more successful than your own. In the absence of such luxuries, however, quite good pancake rolls can be made as follows:

Batter

1¼ cups all-purpose flour
¼ cup tapioca flour or cornstarch
4 eggs
2 cups water
peanut oil

Sift the flour into a bowl. Break in the eggs, and stir lightly, adding the water to produce a thin batter. Heat a little oil in a frying pan, and when it is hot pour in enough batter to cover the bottom of the pan *thinly*. When it is cooked, lift the pancake out and place it on the back of an upturned bread and butter plate to cool. Proceed in the same way until all the batter is used up, piling each successive pancake on top of the last. (The back of the plate method makes it easier to separate the pancakes when you need them later.)

For the filling

½ lb. raw small shrimp, peeled, deveined and roughly chopped
½ lb. pork chop meat, shredded
¼ lb. bean sprouts, with the heads pulled off
1 small bunch Chinese leeks, cut into 1-inch lengths, *or* a good
    handful chives, similarly treated
4 yellow onions, finely chopped
4 cloves garlic, smashed and chopped finely
a few chopped water chestnuts
1 medium white turnip, shredded or grated into fine strips
soya sauce to taste
sugar to taste
peanut oil for frying

Heat 4 tablespoons oil in a wok or a frying pan, and fry the
onions until they are golden. Take them up and set aside. Add a
little more oil, and fry the pork and shrimp until they are cooked.
Remove these from the pan and set aside. Adding more oil to the
pan if necessary, lightly stir-fry the bean sprouts, water chestnuts
and Chinese leeks or chives. Lift these out and set aside. Now
fry the garlic in the pan until it is light brown, then add the turnip
and a dash of water, cover the pan and simmer until the vegetable
is tender. When it is cooked but not soggy, stir in the soya sauce
and sugar to taste.

Place all the separately cooked ingredients in a bowl, mix
them together, spoon sufficient filling on to each pancake and
roll it up, tucking in the ends like an envelope. Seal each roll with
a paste made from a little flour and water mixed together.

Deep-fry the rolls in plenty of hot peanut oil until they are
golden brown. Drain and serve immediately.

SPRING ROLLS II. (Makes about 18 rolls)

For the filling

¼ lb. pork chop meat, shredded
½ lb. raw shrimp, shelled, deveined and roughly chopped

¼ lb. crab meat
½-lb. can of bamboo shoots, drained and cut into fine strips
3 Chinese dried mushrooms, soaked and the hard stems removed
5 green onions complete with their green tops, chopped
a few water chestnuts, chopped
¾ teaspoon green ginger, chopped
1½ teaspoons sugar
a large pinch of monosodium glutamate
1 tablespoon Chinese oyster sauce
1½ teaspoons light soya sauce
1½ teaspoons cornstarch
peanut oil

In 4 tablespoons heated peanut oil, stir-fry the pork, shrimp and crab meat. Add the Chinese mushrooms, sliced, the water chestnuts and bamboo shoots, and then the ginger, sugar, sauces and monosodium glutamate. Stir until everything is lightly cooked. Thicken with cornstarch, add the chopped onion and give the mixture a final stir before removing from the pan.

Fill the spring roll skins and proceed in the same way as in the previous recipe.

EGG ROLLS (Makes 6 rolls)

For the egg wrapper

6 eggs, beaten but not frothy
a little hot peanut oil for greasing the pan

In a greased frying pan over a high heat, make 6 very thin omelettes, one at a time. Pile them as they are cooked on to the back of a plate, as in the recipe for Spring Rolls pancake wrappers.

For the filling

½ lb. minced chicken breast or fine lean ground beef
1 small young carrot, cut into very thin matchsticks
1 small yellow onion, finely chopped
1 red chilli, thinly sliced

179

a few green beans *or* a stick of celery *or*, at a pinch, a small wedge
  of young cabbage, finely shredded
3 or 4 green onions, complete with green tops, finely chopped
1 thick slice green ginger, smashed and chopped
1 tablespoon cornstarch
1 tablespoon light soya sauce
pepper and salt to taste
peanut oil

Mix the chopped meat or chicken with the soya sauce, cornstarch, salt and pepper. Heat a little peanut oil in a pan. Fry the ginger and onions until golden, add the beans, carrots and meat, and stir until the meat changes colour and the vegetables are cooked but not soft (see p. 23). Throw in the green onions and chilli, stir once more. Remove from the pan, divide into 6 portions, and allow to cool.

When the filling is cool, place each portion on an egg round, roll it up, tucking in the corner envelope-style, and seal the edges with a thick flour-and-water paste. The rolls may be either deep fried until brown in plenty of hot oil, or steamed for a few minutes on a rack over boiling water in a covered pan. Serve with salad, whole or sliced in rounds.

EGG FOO YOONG

6 eggs
3 green onions, chopped
$\frac{1}{2}$ can button mushrooms *or* 6 fresh ones, sautéed in butter
2 slices green ginger, chopped
3 oz. of any or all of the following: shredded chicken breast,
  shredded rump steak, crab meat, chopped lobster meat, finely
  diced bacon, cooked green peas
salt and pepper to taste
1–2 tablespoons soya sauce
2 tablespoons peanut oil or lard
green onions for garnish

Heat the oil or lard in a pan. Brown the ginger. Then put in all the other ingredients except the eggs and stir-fry until cooked. Add the eggs, which have been lightly beaten, allow to half set, then stir lightly and leave to set like an omelette and brown on the bottom. Garnish with finely chopped green onions.

BAKED BEAN CURD

8 squares soft bean curd
¼ lb. ground pork
1 clove garlic, finely chopped
1 teaspoon dark soya sauce
2 green onions, chopped
1 stalk celery, chopped
2 eggs
salt and pepper to taste
1 tablespoon peanut oil

Season the pork with the garlic and soya sauce, letting it stand aside until needed. Drain the bean curd and roughly chop it. Put the oil in a pan, and when it is hot stir-fry the seasoned meat until it is brown. Drain. Transfer into a mixing bowl, and stir in the bean curd, adding the eggs, lightly beaten, the green onions and celery. Mix all together well, add salt and pepper and place in a moderate oven in a pyrex dish for 45 minutes, when the mixture should look something like a scrambled egg custard.

STEAMED, DRESSED BEAN CURD

1 lb. soft bean curd, roughly chopped and drained
1 egg white, beaten
1 egg yolk, lightly beaten
¾ teaspoon monosodium glutamate
½ chicken breast, minced
1 chopped green onion
1½ teaspoons ginger juice (see p. 33)
¾ teaspoon dry sherry
salt to taste
½ cup shelled green peas

181

½ cup young carrots, diced
1 or 2 tablespoons sesame oil
2 or slightly more tablespoons cornstarch
¾–1¼ cups water

Mix the bean curd, egg white, salt to taste and ⅜ teaspoon monosodium glutamate in a bowl. In another bowl, thoroughly mix the chicken, egg yolk, green onion, ginger juice, sherry and salt to taste.

Grease the inside of a small bowl or pyrex dish, fill with alternate layers of the bean curd and meat mixtures, and steam, uncovered, on a rack in a covered pan of boiling water for 15 minutes. When it is set, turn out of the dish and keep warm on a large plate.

In the meantime, heat the sesame oil in a pan, and stir-fry the peas and carrots in it till they are well coated. Mix the cornstarch, water, salt and pepper to taste, and the remaining ¼ teaspoon monosodium glutamate. Add this to the pan and, stirring all together, let it simmer until the peas and carrots are lightly cooked and the gravy has thickened. Surround the bean curd mould with this mixture, and serve while still hot.

Indian

CURRY POWDER

A curry is not just a dish made with curry powder. The most trustworthy curry recipes usually specify all the separate ingredients in their individual quantities. But there are some that, along with a number of other things, call for an amount of this ambiguous mixture.

It is important to remember that there are many different possible combinations embraced by the term. For those who wish to have a bulk supply of curry powder in the cupboard to use when it is called for, I am here including two versions. The first one, which contains fennel and lemon grass, can be used for any South East Asian, Ceylon or Malay curry. But for Indian recipes choose only the second, as fennel is never an ingredient of Indian curries.

For 1 lb. meat, use 1–2 tablespoons curry powder. Use less for vegetables.

CEYLON CURRY POWDER

6 oz. coriander seeds
4 oz. cumin seeds
1 oz. fennel seeds
1 oz. mustard seeds
1 oz. fenugreek
a handful of lemon grass and curry leaves, sliced
mustard or peanut oil

Fry the seeds in a small amount of mustard or peanut oil in a pan until they smell cooked. Put in the mustard seeds last of all as they will jump about. Allow to cool, and grind in a blender until they are powdered. Add the lemon grass and curry leaves, stir to mix well and store in a screwtop jar.

INDIAN CURRY POWDER

1 lb. coriander seeds
5 oz. turmeric
2½ oz. peppercorns
2 oz. fenugreek
4 oz. cumin

Fry the seeds lightly in a small amount of oil, grind to a powder in a blender and store when cool in a screwtop jar.

If chilli is not separately specified in a recipe, add ground chilli to taste as you use the curry powders.

VADAY (Ceylon)

This is a particularly good appetizer to serve with drinks or at a cocktail party.

½ lb. lentils or split peas (ooloonthoo)
2 medium yellow onions, finely chopped
2 or 3 green chillies, sliced (the ones you can buy fresh, about
    3 inches long)
a small piece green ginger
oil or ghee for deep frying

Soak the lentils in water overnight. The next day, drain them and grind well in a mortar or blender. Let the ground meal stand for a further hour or so. Then mix in the chopped onions, chillies and chopped green ginger with salt to taste. Form the mixture into balls and flatten on an oiled surface, to prevent sticking. Deep fry until crisp in boiling oil or ghee. Drain on kitchen paper and serve.

For a special occasion, press a peeled whole shrimp into each savoury before deep frying.

FRIED CURRY PUFFS

The pastry for curry puffs can be made with or without coconut milk.

Pastry

2½ cups sifted all-purpose flour
¾ cup thick coconut milk *or* plain milk (perhaps a little less)
¾ teaspoon salt

Mix coconut milk or milk into the flour with salt and lightly knead into a soft dough. Roll out very thinly and cut into circles about 3 inches across.

For the curry filling

½ lb. lean lamb, beef or chicken, finely chopped or minced
1 yellow onion, finely chopped
1 large potato, boiled, peeled and diced
5 teaspoons Indian curry powder (see p. 184)
¾ teaspoon ground chilli
¾ teaspoon roughly ground black pepper
salt
1 tablespoon ghee *or* 2 tablespoons oil
peanut oil for deep frying

Heat the oil in a pan and fry the onion until golden. Add the meat, curry powder, chilli and pepper. Stir until everything is well mixed and the meat has changed colour. Add salt to taste and a little water. Cook for 5 minutes – until the meat is done and the curry is dry. Lastly, add the potatoes and stir thoroughly to mix. Allow to cool.

Place a little filling on each pastry round, fold over into a semi-circle, seal with milk or egg white. Deep fry in plenty of hot peanut oil until golden brown. Drain and serve hot or cool.

MULLIGATAWNY WITH MEAT STOCK (Ceylon)

1 lb. stewing beef with bone
10 cups water
1 lb. yellow onions, finely chopped
20 whole black peppercorns
3-inch-stick cinnamon bark
salt
3 large, ripe tomatoes, skinned
$\frac{3}{4}$ teaspoon ground chilli (or more if you prefer it hotter)
a pinch of turmeric
1 tablespoon Ceylon curry powder (see p. 183)
10 cloves garlic, peeled and bruised
8 slices green ginger
2 stalks celery
a few curry leaves
1 stalk lemon grass, bruised
3 large potatoes, peeled and diced
$1\frac{1}{4}$ cups thick coconut milk
$\frac{1}{4}$ lb. ($\frac{1}{2}$ cup) ghee
juice of 1 lime or small lemon

Cut the beef into cubes and simmer in the water for 2 hours with salt, peppercorns and cinnamon bark. Then add half the onions, the chopped tomatoes, potatoes, celery, chilli, curry powder, turmeric, garlic, ginger, some of the curry leaves and the lemon grass.

After another 2 hours of gentle simmering the water should have reduced by half. Now add the coconut milk. Sauté the remaining onions and curry leaves in the ghee until light brown and add this to the pot. Stir well and strain off the liquid, pressing the potatoes through the strainer and squeezing the goodness out of the meat. Add lemon juice and serve hot.

ABGOOSHTH

This is an Indian Moslem dish. It can be served with other courses as a very substantial soup, or would make an adequate family meal on its own accompanied only by thick chunks of crusty white bread and butter and a bowl of salad.

3 thick chops (about 1 inch through), cut from the end of a leg of
  lamb through the bone
3 medium-size yellow onions, chopped
¾ lb. 'chanai' lentils or yellow split peas
4 big ripe tomatoes, skinned and chopped
1 stick cinnamon bark
4 or 5 cardamom seeds, broken open
4 or 5 whole cloves
1 lime *or* ¼ green lemon with the skin attached
a few whole peppercorns
salt to taste
2 medium eggplants
butter
1 large bunch mint for garnish

Cut each chop into three, leaving in the bone. Put the pieces of meat and all the other ingredients except the eggplants, lemon and mint into a large saucepan. Add 12½–15 cups of water, bring to the boil, then lower the heat, cover, and simmer the pot until the lentils are soft and cooked.

Just before removing from the fire, put in the whole piece of lemon and then stir in the chopped mint. Meanwhile, slice the eggplants into thick rounds and fry the slices in butter until brown.

Pour the contents of the saucepan into a large tureen. Remove the lemon, float the browned eggplant slices on top of the soup, and serve at the table.

COARSE FISH CURRY (Ceylon)

The shark, or flake, is a fish often despised by angler and house-wife alike. But it really makes good eating, and is just the thing for this curry.

1 lb. shark or flake (mackerel, mullet, ocean perch can also be used)

1 tablespoon ground chilli
1½ teaspoons turmeric
1½ teaspoons mustard seed
2 green chillies, sliced
2 cloves garlic
3 slices green ginger
a few curry leaves
1-inch-stalk lemon grass, finely sliced
½ cup thick coconut milk
1 yellow onion, chopped
a dash of white vinegar
salt to taste
2 tablespoons coconut or vegetable oil

Cut fish into chunks and poach in a little water with salt and vinegar added. When it is cooked, remove the fish for use and keep the stock aside. Grind the mustard, ginger and garlic together in a mortar. Spread this mixture over the fish, and keep this aside too.

Heat the coconut or vegetable oil and fry the onion, lemon grass and curry leaves until they are golden brown. Add the rest of the spices including the green chillies, then the seasoned fish. Stir gently, and allow to dry for a few minutes. Lower the heat, add the fish stock, and bring back to simmering point. Add thick coconut milk, stir and serve.

DRY FISH CURRY

This recipe comes from Mrs. Wilhelmina Sim of Kuching, who supplies recipes every month for the Women's Institute Radio Programme of Malaysia.

1 lb. fish steaks (salmon, mackerel, mullet, Spanish mackerel, pompano, snapper)
2 yellow onions, finely chopped and the excess moisture squeezed out
½-inch-piece green ginger, smashed and chopped
2 cloves garlic, finely chopped

4 curry leaves
½ cup tamarind water made from a walnut-sized piece of tamarind
   pulp
2 tablespoons coriander seeds
1 tablespoon cumin seeds
12 dried hot chillies
1½ teaspoons turmeric
1½ teaspoons peppercorns
1½ teaspoons mustard seeds
5 tablespoons vegetable oil
salt to taste

Grind the coriander, cumin, chillies, turmeric, mustard seed's
and peppercorns to a powder in a blender. Heat the oil in a
saucepan. Fry the garlic and onions until golden brown. Add
the ground ingredients and fry until fragrant. Now add the ginger
and curry leaves, salt and tamarind water. Stir well and allow
to boil, then add the fish. Cover the pan and simmer gently for
5 minutes. Then stir carefully until the fish is cooked and the
gravy is thick, when it is ready to serve.

FRIED SHRIMP CURRY (A Dry Curry)

1 lb. uncooked jumbo shrimp
2 medium new potatoes, lightly cooked and diced
4 tablespoons peanut or other vegetable oil
½ medium yellow onion, grated or chopped fine and the excess
   moisture squeezed out
1 tablespoon ground chilli
2 teaspoons ground turmeric
1½ teaspoons fennel seeds
¾ teaspoon coriander seeds
1-inch stick cinnamon
3 curry leaves, chopped
1 cup thick coconut milk
a dash of paprika for colour (optional, not at all authentic, but
   sometimes necessary as a substitute for explosive amounts of
   chilli)

189

Heat 2 tablespoons oil in a pan or a wok. Put in the shrimp, which have been deveined and shelled to the tail but with the tail left on, and fry them, stirring constantly until they are cooked. Add the ground chilli and turmeric and stir some more until the shrimp are well coated with the spices, then lift everything out and set aside. Add the remaining oil to the pan and fry the onion until golden brown. (It is important to use finely chopped or grated onion which has been squeezed dry before going into the pan as the aim is to avoid a thick gravy.)

In a separate pan, lightly roast the coriander and fennel seeds, then grind to a powder in a blender. Add these spices to the curry pan and then the coconut milk. Stir together, and cook the resultant sauce *uncovered* until it has reduced almost entirely and the oil has separated from the spices, which are now half-frying in a mass.

Now add the shrimp and the cooked potato cubes, and stir well until the solids are thoroughly coated with curry mixture and the whole dry curry is frying in its own oil.

Lastly stir in the chopped curry leaves and ground cinnamon, with a dash of paprika, stir again, and the curry is ready.

CHICKEN CURRY I

1 chicken cut into curry pieces (see p. 24)
1 tablespoon coriander seeds
10 dried chillies
1 tablespoon turmeric
$\frac{1}{2}$-inch-piece green ginger, smashed and chopped
3 cloves garlic, smashed and chopped
2 yellow onions, chopped
$\frac{3}{4}$ teaspoon cumin seeds
$\frac{3}{4}$ teaspoon black pepper
1-inch-piece cinnamon bark
$\frac{3}{8}$ teaspoon fenugreek
2 cups thin coconut milk
$\frac{1}{2}$ cup thick coconut milk

salt to taste
1 tablespoon ghee
juice of $\frac{1}{4}$ lemon (optional)

Grind all the dry spices except fenugreek and cinnamon to a powder in a blender. Fry them in a little ghee until they smell cooked, then remove from the pan and mix thoroughly with the chicken pieces. Leave the spiced chicken aside for the present.

Heat the rest of the ghee, and put in the onions, garlic, ginger, fenugreek and cinnamon and fry until the onions are soft. Now add thin coconut milk and stir as it comes to the boil. Add the spiced chicken, stir thoroughly, turn down the heat, and simmer uncovered until the chicken is tender. When it is cooked, add the thick coconut milk and return to the boil, then remove from the fire.

The juice of $\frac{1}{4}$ lemon may be added just before serving, according to taste.

CHICKEN CURRY II (A Dry Curry)

1 chicken, cut into curry pieces (see p. 24)
1 tablespoon ground coriander
1 tablespoon ground chilli
$\frac{3}{4}$ teaspoon turmeric
$1\frac{1}{2}$ cups thick coconut milk
1 large onion, finely chopped
$1\frac{1}{2}$ teaspoons fennel seeds
a few curry leaves
1 tablespoon ghee

Mix the coriander, chilli, and turmeric with the chicken pieces. Put the coconut milk in a saucepan and bring to the boil. Drop in the spiced chicken and allow to simmer, uncovered, until the chicken is tender and the gravy is reduced, forming a dry curry.

In the meantime, heat the ghee in another pan, and when it is hot add the onion, the fennel seeds, which have been roughly broken in a mortar but not ground, and the curry leaves. Fry to golden brown and add to the chicken curry. Stir and serve.

191

CHICKEN CURRY III (Ceylon)

1 chicken cut into curry pieces (see p. 24)
2-inch-piece green ginger, smashed and chopped
2 large cloves garlic, smashed and chopped
2 yellow onions, chopped
4 fresh green chillies, sliced
1 stalk lemon grass, finely sliced
a few curry leaves
1½ teaspoons turmeric
salt
2 cups thin coconut milk
1 cup thick coconut milk
1 tablespoon ghee or butter
shavings of Maldive fish *or* 6 dried shrimp previously roasted in a
frying pan and roughly chopped when cool (optional)

Rub the chicken pieces well with turmeric and salt. Lightly
sauté the fresh spices, onions and garlic in ghee until they smell
cooked. Add the chicken and brown, then add the thin coconut
milk and simmer. When the chicken is tender, add the thick
coconut milk and reheat for a few minutes until well blended.

Sometimes people like to sprinkle shavings of Maldive fish
over this curry. If you cannot get hold of this popular Ceylonese
curry accompaniment, try dried shrimp prepared in the way I
have suggested.

A RICH CHICKEN CURRY (Ceylon)

1 chicken cut into curry pieces (see p. 24)
1 tablespoon turmeric
1 large yellow onion, grated
2 cloves garlic, crushed
1-inch-piece green ginger, scraped and chopped
1 stalk lemon grass
a few curry leaves
2 teaspoons ground chilli

192

1¼ teaspoons coriander seeds
¾ teaspoon cumin seeds
a pinch of fennel seeds } or 1 tablespoon Ceylon
a pinch of mustard seeds curry powder
a small pinch of fenugreek seeds
4½ teaspoons roughly ground black pepper
1 tablespoon brown sugar
a few crushed cardamom pods
salt to taste
2 cups thin coconut milk
1 cup thick coconut milk
juice of ½ lemon

Rub the chicken pieces all over with the turmeric and leave aside for 30 minutes. F he seeds in a pan in a small amount of hot vegetable oil t they smell cooked. Put the mustard seeds in last, as they wil ump about. Throw in the lemon grass and curry leaves. Wh they are cooked, grind this mixture to a rough powder in blender.

Bring the th coconut milk to the boil in a saucepan. Add all the other fres d ground spices, the onions, garlic and sugar and mix we' dd the seasoned chicken pieces and allow to simmer un red until the chicken is cooked. Then add the thick cocon milk and cook for a further 10 minutes. Just before serving, sti in the lemon juice.

MEAT CURRY (Indian)

1 lb. leg of lamb chops
2 or 3 yellow onions, chopped
4 cloves garlic, smashed and chopped
4 thin slices green ginger, smashed and chopped
2 tablespoons Indian curry powder (see p. 184)
3 cardamom pods
3 cloves
1-inch-piece cinnamon bark
salt
1 tomato, chopped
2 tablespoons ghee *or* butter or mustard oil

Pound the cardamom, cloves and cinnamon roughly in a mortar. Fry the chopped onions in hot ghee until they are soft. Add the garlic and ginger and fry until they smell cooked. Put in the meat and brown it, then the curry powder, cardamom, cloves and cinnamon. Stir well to mix, add salt and a little water. Cook for a few minutes on a high heat, then turn the stove low and simmer, covered, until the meat is half cooked (about 30 minutes). Add the tomato, finish cooking and serve.

LAMB KURMAH

1½ lbs. lamb (2 thick slices with the bone left in, sawn from the end
   of the leg)
2 yellow onions, chopped
1½ teaspoons ground chilli
1½ teaspoons coriander seeds
3 cloves garlic, chopped
5 cardamom pods
4 cloves
3-inch-stick cinnamon
1½ teaspoons turmeric
2 teaspoons salt
6 tablespoons butter or ghee
1 container (1 cup) yoghurt

Dice the meat into 1-inch cubes. Grind the dry seeds and spices to a powder in an electric blender or a mortar. Heat the butter in a saucepan and fry the onions until they are light brown. Add the ground spices and garlic and then the pieces of meat. Thoroughly stir and mix the contents of the pot, then add the yoghurt, stirring again. Cover the saucepan and simmer until the meat is tender, adding a little water if necessary as the kurmah should not be allowed to cook dry.

MRS. NAIR'S DRY CURRY (THORAN)

This curry comes from Malabar via Malaya. It is not at all unlike the Malay *rendang* (see p. 91)

1 lb. boned leg of lamb, cubed
2 yellow onions, chopped
2 large cloves garlic, crushed
2 thick slices green ginger, chopped
1½ teaspoons ground hot chilli
1 tablespoon butter or ghee
2 tablespoons coriander seeds
⅜ teaspoon ground black pepper
½ fresh coconut, grated
3 curry leaves

Mix the meat with the chilli and leave aside. Fry 1½ onions, the garlic and ginger in the melted butter or ghee until soft. Then put in the meat and chilli, add a little water, and allow to cook uncovered on a medium fire until the meat is tender and the curry is dry.

In the meantime roast the coriander seeds in a greased frying pan and grind them. Add the coriander and the pepper to the cooked-meat mixture and stir. Mix together the grated coconut, the remaining finely chopped onion and the chopped curry leaves. Add these to the curry, with salt to taste, stir well, and cook for a few minutes more, when it will be ready to serve.

SHAMI KEBABS (Moslem)

½ lb. ground meat with no fat (leg of lamb or rump steak)
½ lb. yellow lentils or split peas
2 yellow onions, finely chopped
5 cardamom pods
5 cloves
1-inch-stick cinnamon

a handful of mint leaves, chopped
pepper and salt to taste
2 eggs

Cover the lentils with water and boil them until they are soft –
about 45 minutes to 1 hour. Drain them well. Add the ground
meat and the onions, stir together and cook without adding
any water or oil until the meat is done and the mixture is hashed
and dry. Grind the cardamom pods, cinnamon and cloves to a
powder, and put them in a bowl with the meat and lentils mixture.
Now mash everything together into a thick paste, adding salt
and pepper to taste. Beat the eggs, and stir them in. Add the
chopped mint. Shape the mixture into patties, and fry. Serve
with salad.

KHEEMA (Moslem)

1 lb. uncooked leg of lamb or beef
1½ yellow onions, chopped
2-inch-stick cinnamon
6 cardamom pods
6 cloves
1½ teaspoons chopped garlic
2 teaspoons chopped green ginger
a pinch of ground turmeric
2 large ripe tomatoes, peeled and chopped
2 tablespoons butter or ghee
salt to taste

Trim the meat of all fat and chop it small. Grind the cinnamon,
cardamom and cloves to a powder in a blender or with a mortar
and pestle. Heat the butter in a heavy saucepan and fry the onions
until they are golden brown. Add the green ginger, garlic, turmeric and the ground spices, stir, and fry them all together for 1
minute. Now put in the meat, and mix everything together well.
Cover the saucepan, turn the stove down low and cook the meat
for about 30 minutes without adding any extra water. When it is
done, add the chopped tomatoes and salt to taste. Replace the

lid and cook for a little longer. (Just before serving, small new potatoes that have been boiled in their skins may be stirred into the kheema.)

Serve kheema with kitchedi (see p. 205), chutney, raita (yoghurt with chopped celery mixed into it) and a salad of lettuce, tomato, and cucumber slices, with or without an oil and vinegar dressing.

DHALL CURRY (Ceylon)

½ lb. dhall or lentils
2 cups water
1 cup thick coconut milk
1 green chilli, sliced
⅜ teaspoon ground cumin seeds
¾ teaspoon roughly ground peppercorns
⅜ teaspoon turmeric
1 onion, finely chopped
1 clove garlic, crushed

Wash the lentils well. Boil them in water to which has been added the onions, chillies, garlic and turmeric. When they are cooked, add the coconut milk and bring back to the boil. Add peppercorns, cumin and salt to taste. Stir well and serve.

DHALL EGG CURRY

5 hard-boiled eggs
½ lb. lentils
salt
2 yellow onions
4 tablespoons ghee or butter
2 tablespoons Indian curry powder (see p. 184)

Soak the lentils in cold water overnight. Fry the sliced onions in a saucepan until golden brown. Add the curry powder, mix well and add the lentils. Cook this for 5 minutes stirring all the time.

197

Then add a scant ¾ cup of hot water. Season with salt and simmer till the lentils are tender and have absorbed all the water. Cut the hard-boiled eggs into halves and add to the lentils a few minutes before serving.

BRINJAL (EGGPLANT) WHITE CURRY

2 medium eggplants, skinned and diced
2 yellow onions, chopped
1 large clove garlic, crushed
4 green chillies, sliced in rounds with their seeds
¾ teaspoon fenugreek, roughly broken in a mortar
1½ teaspoons turmeric
1½ cups thick coconut milk
a few uncooked shrimp, peeled and deveined (optional)
salt to taste

Place the chillies, onions, garlic, turmeric, fenugreek and shrimp (if used) in the bottom of a saucepan. Then put in the eggplants and pour the coconut milk over the top. Do not stir, but cover and cook over a low fire. Stir the pot when the vegetable is half cooked and return to the stove until it is tender and ready to serve.

BRINJAL (EGGPLANT) CURRY (Ceylon)

2 medium eggplants
1 yellow onion, chopped
1 clove garlic, finely sliced
¾ teaspoon ground chilli
1 tablespoon Ceylon curry powder (see p. 183)
1 cup thick coconut milk
1 tablespoon white vinegar
a little turmeric
salt to taste
coconut or other vegetable oil

198

Cut the unpeeled eggplants into thin slices lengthwise. Sprinkle each slice with a little turmeric and salt. Heat some oil in a pan and fry the slices until they are beginning to brown. Drain.

In another pan fry the onion and garlic in a little oil until they are soft. Add curry powder and chilli and mix well. Add the coconut milk and boil until it is thick. Add the eggplant and let it simmer for a few minutes. Finally add the vinegar and cook, stirring on a low heat, until the gravy has become very thick.

POTATO PATCHELLI (South Indian)

4 Idaho potatoes, boiled, drained and *roughly* mashed
3 or 4 fresh green chillies, seeds removed and finely chopped
1 large yellow onion, finely chopped
1 slice green ginger, smashed and chopped
thick coconut milk
salt to taste
¾ cup yoghurt, beaten

Mix the potatoes, chillies, onion and ginger together, and add the thick coconut milk stirring until everything assumes the consistency of thick porridge. Add salt to taste, then the beaten yoghurt and mix well. Put on the stove, bring to the boil, and serve.

As a variation you can add just before serving a few curry leaves, a little mustard seed and 2 dried chillies that have been fried and then roughly ground. Patchelli, or pachadi, is the southern counterpart of the North Indian *raita*.

ZUCCHINI PACHADI (Malabar)

¼ (or 3-inch slice) large zucchini, peeled and diced
6 green chillies, chopped fine, *or* 1½ teaspoons ground chilli
a few curry leaves
½ fresh coconut, ground, *or* ½ cup dried grated coconut
1 tablespoon mustard seed, roughly broken in a mortar
1 cup good thick, sour yoghurt, three days old
extra mustard seed, dried chilli, curry leaves, coconut, ghee

199

Mix the chopped green chillies with the zucchini. Add salt to taste. Put them in a saucepan and add just enough boiling water to cook the zucchini. (It only takes a little in the bottom of the pan. If any is left by the time the zucchini is cooked, drain it off.) When the zucchini is tender, add the curry leaves, remove the saucepan from the fire, cover, and leave aside. Beat the yoghurt, mustard seed and coconut together. Pour this over the vegetable and mix well.

Take another handful of coconut, mix it with a little roughly broken mustard seed, chopped dried chilli and curry leaves. Fry this mixture in a little ghee and add to the vegetable. Stir again, reheat and serve.

VEGETABLE CURRY (Ceylon)

6 small zucchini
12 pickling onions *or* 3 medium yellow onions, quartered
3 fresh chillies
1 tablespoon curry powder (see p. 183)
1 cup thick coconut milk
½ cup thin coconut milk
tamarind water made from a piece of tamarind the size of a walnut
   (see p. 37)
a few peppercorns
ghee for frying
salt to taste

Scrape but do not peel the zucchini. Slice them into rounds about 1 inch thick. Sauté the sliced chillies and the pickling onions whole. Then put all the ingredients into a saucepan, bring to the boil and simmer until cooked.

CABBAGE WHITE CURRY (or Any Green Vegetable)

1 small cabbage, finely shredded, *or* 1 lb. green beans cut into
   ¼-inch lengths
2 onions, finely chopped

2 cloves garlic, crushed
1 slice green ginger, finely chopped
5 green chillies
a small pinch of turmeric
a few curry leaves
¾ teaspoon mustard seed
1 tablespoon dried grated coconut
a little ghee
½ cup thick coconut milk

Mix the vegetable with the dried coconut, onions, garlic, ginger green chillies, turmeric and salt. Heat 2 teaspoons of ghee in a pan and fry the curry leaves and mustard seed until they are cooked. Add the vegetable mixture and fry for 1 minute, stirring all the while. Add a very small amount of water and cook the cabbage until it is tender but not soggy. At the end of the cooking add the coconut milk, let it come to the boil, and serve.

CABBAGE MALLUN (Ceylon)

the green, outer leaves of a cabbage, finely shredded
1 yellow onion, finely sliced
3 green chillies, sliced *or* 1 teaspoon ground chilli
2 tablespoons dried grated coconut
a pinch of turmeric

Put the cabbage, onion, chillies and salt into a covered saucepan without water and cook on a quick fire. (If the cabbage is allowed to cook slowly the water will come out and the vegetable will lose its greenness.) Do not overcook as the cabbage should remain slightly crisp. When it is done, add the coconut which has been previously mixed with a pinch of turmeric. Toss well and continue cooking, stirring all the time. When the coconut smells cooked the dish is ready.

AVIAL (VEGETABLE CURRY) (Malabar)

For this liquid curry you can use cabbage, green beans, okra, tomatoes, potatoes or in fact any vegetable either on its own or in combination.

enough vegetable for 2 or 3 people
4 or 5 green chillies, sliced in half
salt to taste
1 container (1 cup) yoghurt
½ fresh coconut, grated, *or* ½ cup dried grated coconut
a small pinch of turmeric

Mix the vegetable and chillies together, adding salt to taste and a little turmeric for colour. Add just enough water to cook the vegetable. When it is cooked do not drain but add the yoghurt which has been mixed with the coconut. Stir well, bring back to the boil and serve.

TOMATO CURRY (Ceylon)

1 lb. ripe tomatoes, skinned
1½ teaspoons chilli powder
1 tablespoon dried shrimp, roasted and ground
1 tablespoon dried grated coconut
3 cloves garlic, sliced
2 yellow onions, sliced
a piece of lemon grass, finely sliced
a few curry leaves

Mix all ingredients together and cook to a pulp.

SEENI SAMBOL (Ceylon) (Serves about 10)

This is a curry accompaniment which is eaten on special occasions. It is very rich and *very* hot. Seeni sambol should ideally be prepared about two days before it is to be eaten. If you do this, however, do not add the coconut milk until the day it is to be used.

4 lbs. yellow onions, finely sliced
a few stalks of lemon grass
a handful of curry leaves
pieces of cinnamon bark
tamarind water made from a large nut of tamarind pulp (see p. 37)
4 tablespoons ground chilli, freshly made from dried hot chillies roasted in a pan and ground in a blender
a few cardamom seeds, roughly broken
½ lb. or more dried shrimp, roughly broken in a blender
salt to taste
1 tablespoon sugar
about 8 cups thick coconut milk
coconut oil

Heat the oil in a pan until it is very hot. Add the sliced onions, shrimp, lemon grass and curry leaves and fry until light brown. Add all the other spices and stir until they smell cooked. Add the coconut milk, sugar and tamarind water and boil until the sambol is thick and the oil is floating on top.

To give hamburgers or hot dogs a real lift, smear them with seeni sambol instead of mustard. Try it as a relish with barbecued chops or steak.

COCONUT SAMBOL (Ceylon)

There are many varieties of sambols. They are served as an accompaniment to a main dish. Any fruit or vegetable can be treated in this way, using either coconut or coconut milk.

the scraped flesh of 1 fresh coconut *or* ½ lb. dried grated coconut, moistened with water
1 tablespoon ground chilli powder
2 tablespoons sliced yellow onion
juice of 1 lemon
salt

Mix all the ingredients together, adding the lemon juice last, then serve. As a variation add 2 teaspoons dried shrimp, which have been previously roasted and ground in a blender.

PINEAPPLE PICKLE

1 medium pineapple
1 tablespoon ground chilli powder
1 tablespoon mustard seed
1 clove garlic
2 slices green ginger
a pinch of turmeric
a scant cup good white vinegar
salt to taste

Peel the pineapple and dice it. Grind all the spices with a little vinegar. Mix in the remaining vinegar, add the pineapple and salt and mix well together. This pickle can be eaten straight away, and should not be kept more than 2 or 3 days.

EGGPLANT PICKLE (Ceylon)

1 medium eggplant
4 green chillies, cut in half
1 clove garlic, sliced
a scant cup good white vinegar
a pinch of turmeric
1 tablespoon mustard seed
salt
coconut oil

Cut the eggplant into thin slices lengthwise. Fry these in oil on both sides until brown. Add the chillies and garlic and half-fry. Drain off any excess oil and mix in the other spices which have been ground to a paste in a little vinegar. Add the rest of the vinegar, salt to taste, and leave for two or three days. Eat the pickle within a week.

204

TOMATO CHUTNEY (Indian)

4 large, ripe tomatoes, skinned and diced
4 green chillies, finely chopped
1 large yellow onion, finely chopped
5 tablespoons thick coconut milk

Mix everything together and simmer gently until the ingredients are soft, adding a little water if necessary. Mash thoroughly, add the coconut milk, return to the boil and serve.

KITCHEDI (Serves 10 as an accompaniment to curries, 6 as a luncheon dish) (South Indian)

$\frac{1}{2}$ lb. Masoor dhall or red lentils, washed and soaked in water for at
  least 1 hour, then drained
1$\frac{1}{4}$ lbs. good long-grain rice, preferably Patna
4 tablespoons butter or ghee
2 large yellow onions, chopped
2 or 3 cloves garlic, crushed
1-inch-piece green ginger, smashed and chopped
a small pinch of turmeric
2 or 3 cardamom pods, broken open in a mortar
2-inch-stick cinnamon bark
3 or 4 cloves
a few whole peppercorns

For garnish

6 tablespoons chopped green leaves of chopped green onion,
  mint or parsley
2 hard-boiled eggs

Tie the cardamom, cinnamon, cloves and peppercorns in a small square of muslin and put aside for later use. Thoroughly wash the rice and the dhall separately in a sieve until the water draining out is clear. Put the butter on the stove in a good heavy saucepan, and when it is hot fry the onions, ginger, garlic and turmeric until they are soft. Then stir in the thoroughly drained rice, and

205

fry it, stirring all the time, until it loses its opaque whiteness and becomes yellowish and clear. Now add just under 6½ cups boiling water and let it boil fast on the stove without a lid. When the rice is half cooked (about 5–10 minutes), add the drained dhall and the muslin bag of spices. Let the pot continue to bubble until the water is just disappearing from the surface, then take the saucepan off the stove, cover it with a tight-fitting lid, wrap it completely in two bathtowels and leave it to cook in its own steam for an hour or so.

Before serving, spoon the rice and dhall mixture out into a big bowl, remove the bag of spices and discard it, and garnish the dish with slices of hard-boiled egg and chopped green leaves of green onion. Kitchedi usually goes with North Indian meat curries but is quite elegant enough to serve alone as a luncheon dish.

Miscellaneous Malaysian

MALAYSIAN CANAPÉS AND COCKTAIL SAVOURIES

FRIED SHRIMP PASTE ROUNDS OR
SHRIMP PASTE BALLS

Cut white bread without the crust into savoury-sized rounds. Spread on them the shrimp paste described in the recipe for Kai Choy with Shrimp (see p. 170) and garnish with strips of ham, pressed on top. Deep fry the savoury rounds in plenty of boiling peanut oil. Drain and serve hot or cold.

Alternatively, roll the same shrimp paste mixture into balls. Coat with broken Chinese vermicelli or chopped almonds, and deep-fry.

CHRYS TEH'S COCKTAIL CIRCLETS

1 cup all-purpose flour, sifted
2 tablespoons butter or margarine
¾ teaspoon salt
2 large eggs
1 oz. dried shrimp, finely chopped in a blender
1 onion, very finely sliced
2 fresh chillies, seeds removed, finely chopped or minced
peanut oil for deep frying

Add salt and the butter cut into small pieces to the flour and rub together until the mixture is crumbly. Mix in the egg and knead the dough lightly. Add the chopped shrimp, onions and chillies. Gather up the mixture into a ball and leave it for 10 minutes. Then roll out the dough thinly and cut into biscuit shapes, straws or circles. Deep-fry in hot oil until golden. Store in tightly covered cans.

207

MALAYSIAN SANDWICH

6 oz. dried shrimp
3 yellow onions
2 fresh chillies
4 tablespoons peanut oil

Soak the dried shrimp in water for 10 minutes. Drain. Finely mash them with the chillies in a blender. Finely chop the onions. Heat the oil in a pan and fry the onions until they are light brown. Turn down the heat and add the mashed shrimp and chilli and stir. Fry everything until brown. Remove and allow to cool. Make into white bread sandwiches and cut them into triangles.

FRIED MEAT PATTIES WITH CHINESE PASTRY

For the pastry

3 cups all-purpose flour, sifted
about 2 cups boiling water

To make the pastry, mix the flour with the boiling water and knead until the dough is smooth and non-sticky. Allow to rest for 15 minutes.

For the filling

$\frac{1}{2}$ lb. lean beef or chicken, finely chopped or ground
2 onions, finely chopped
a few Chinese leeks, finely chopped (optional)
4 green onions, including the green part, chopped
1 tablespoon finely chopped green ginger
soya sauce and pepper to taste
$1\frac{1}{2}$ teaspoons sherry
4 tablespoons peanut oil
oil for deep frying

Heat the peanut oil in a pan. Fry the ginger, onions and leeks until lightly brown. Add the meat and stir-fry until it is cooked.

Add the green onions, soya sauce, sherry and seasoning. Stir, remove from the pan and allow to cool.

Roll out the dough. Cut it into small circles, and spoon a little filling onto each. Fold over, pressing the edges together, and form into crescent shapes. Deep fry in plenty of hot oil. Drain and serve with a bowl of chilli sauce to dip into.

SAVOURY POTATO ROLLS

For the potato jacket

4 tablespoons (¼ cup) butter
1 cup all-purpose flour
1 cup water
½ lb. potatoes, boiled and mashed
1 egg
1½ teaspoons salt

Boil the butter and water together in a saucepan. Sift in the flour and salt and beat the mixture well. Cook until the mixture leaves the sides of the pan. Take the saucepan off the stove and gradually beat in the egg. Add the mashed potato and mix well until finely blended. Leave aside.

For the filling

⅜ lb. finely chopped lean beef or chicken
1 onion, chopped
2 cloves garlic, smashed and chopped
2 teaspoons ground coriander
1 tablespoon light soya sauce
¾ teaspoon sugar
salt and pepper to taste
2 tablespoons peanut oil
1 beaten egg
bread crumbs
oil for deep frying

Mix the meat with soya sauce, sugar, coriander, salt and pepper. Heat the oil in a pan and fry the garlic and onion until light brown.

Add the seasoned meat and stir-fry until cooked. Remove from the pan and allow to cool. Take about a tablespoon of the potato mixture and mould it in your hands into a flat round. Place a little cooked filling in the centre and fold and roll the mould around the filling to make little balls. Dip each roll into lightly beaten egg, coat with breadcrumbs and deep-fry in plenty of hot oil until golden brown.

CURRY PATTIES

For the pastry

½ lb. (1 cup) butter or margarine
3 cups all-purpose flour
3 tablespoons water

Cut the butter into small pieces and rub into the flour until thoroughly mixed. Add water slowly, stirring lightly, until you have a thick dough. Gather up into a ball, cover with a damp cloth and leave aside.

For the filling

½ lb. beef or mutton, chopped
2 yellow onions, chopped
2 potatoes, lightly cooked and diced
2 tablespoons oil
5 teaspoons Indian or Ceylon curry powder (see pp. 183–4)
2 teaspoons ground chilli
4 tablespoons water
salt and pepper to taste

Add the curry powder, chilli, salt and pepper to the meat and leave aside. Heat the oil in a pan and fry the onions until they are light brown. Add the seasoned meat and stir until the meat changes colour. Then add the potatoes and water, stir and simmer until the meat is cooked and the curry dry. Leave aside to cool.

Now roll out the dough to about ⅛ inch thick. Cut it into rounds with a pastry cutter. Place a portion of the curry mixture on to each round. Fold over into a semi-circle and seal the edges with a

210

fork. Brush the patties lightly with beaten egg, place on a tray and bake in a hot oven (400° F.) for about 30 minutes or until done.

BROILED SKEWERED SHRIMP OR CRAYFISH

18 raw jumbo shrimp *or* 6 crayfish
4 tablespoons light soya sauce
¾ teaspoon salt
2 teaspoons ginger juice (see p. 33)
5 teaspoons dry sherry
1 tablespoon sugar
peanut oil

Wash, peel and devein the shrimp, leaving the tails intact Chinese-style. Mix everything else in a large bowl and marinate the shrimp in this mixture for 1 hour.

Take 6 skewers or satay sticks and thread 3 shrimp or 1 crayfish on to each. Brush well with peanut oil and broil under an electric broiler, brushing with more oil as the shrimp cook if they look like drying out.

VELVET CRAB ON CRISP VERMICELLI NEST

5 oz. crab meat
3 oz. fresh mushrooms, sliced
¼ lb. green beans, sliced
1 carrot, diced
2 eggs, beaten lightly
2 cloves garlic, finely chopped
1 cup water
¼ cup light cream or evaporated milk
1 tablespoon cornstarch
¾ teaspoon sugar
salt and pepper to taste
¼ lb. Chinese vermicelli (unsoaked)
peanut oil for deep frying

Deep-fry the vermicelli until it is crisp. Drain and spread in a nest shape on a large plate.

Heat 2 tablespoons oil in a saucepan and fry the garlic until it is light brown. Add the beans and carrot and stir-fry until tender. Add the mushrooms, stir and cook a little. Dish up and keep warm.

Mix the water, cream, cornstarch, sugar, salt and pepper together. Pour them into the hot pan. Add the beaten eggs and cook, stirring all the time, until the sauce is thick. Add the crab meat and stir. Pour this over the vermicelli nest with the beans, carrots and mushrooms. Serve immediately.

CHICKEN AND ASPARAGUS

1 chicken breast, sliced
1 can asparagus spears or pieces
$\frac{1}{2}$ of the asparagus water
1 tablespoon light soya sauce
$1\frac{1}{2}$ teaspoons ginger juice (see p. 33)
$\frac{3}{8}$ teaspoon monosodium glutamate
2 heaping tablespoons all-purpose flour
$\frac{1}{2}$ cup light cream
$1\frac{1}{2}$ teaspoons chopped garlic
1 tablespoon peanut oil
salt and pepper to taste

Mix together the ginger juice, soya sauce, monosodium glutamate, salt and pepper. Season the chicken with this and leave aside for 30 minutes.

Heat the peanut oil in a pan and stir-fry the chicken until it is cooked. Take a clean saucepan, heat a little more oil in it and fry the garlic until it is light brown. Stir in the flour and let it fry a little. Slowly add the cream and the asparagus water, stirring all the time until you have a smooth sauce. Now add the chicken slices and asparagus. Return to simmering point, and serve.

MEAT ROLLS

1 lb. pork or beef, cut crossways into broad, thin slices
¼ lb. pork liver, lightly steamed or poached and thinly sliced
⅛ lb. lean bacon, cut into similar-sized strips
½ can bamboo shoots, sliced
1 tablespoon salt
1 tablespoon dark soya sauce
1 tablespoon sugar
1 tablespoon dry sherry
1½ teaspoons ginger juice (see p. 33)
a dash of pepper
1 tablespoon cornstarch

Mix together the salt, soya sauce, sugar, sherry, ginger juice, pepper and cornstarch, and marinate the pork or beef slices in this for 30 minutes.

Spread each meat slice flat, place strips of bacon, liver and bamboo shoots over them, roll up and skewer with a toothpick. Heat a little oil in a pan and fry the rolls until they are brown. Serve with chilli sauce.

MALAYSIAN HAMBURGERS

1 lb. ground beef
3 cloves garlic, crushed
1½ teaspoons cornstarch
dark soya sauce to taste
1½ teaspoons sugar *or* sherry
2 large onions, cut into thick rings
1 tablespoon cornstarch to sprinkle over onion rings
5 or 6 eggs
6 rounds of toast

Mix the garlic, cornstarch, soya sauce, and sugar or sherry together and season the hamburger with this. Stand aside for 15 minutes. Sprinkle some cornstarch over the onion rings and leave them aside.

213

Divide the hamburger into 6 portions, roll into balls and broil on a hot cast-iron pan, flattening each round before you cook it. In the meantime fry the onion rings in hot oil in another pan. Fry the eggs.

Place each hamburger on a slice of toast or lightly toasted bun, top it with an onion ring then a fried egg. Serve with chilli sauce.

BRAISED STEAK AND HARD-BOILED EGGS

1 lb. braising steak, cut into large chunks
5 slices ginger
3 cloves garlic, crushed
5 tablespoons light soya sauce
2 tablespoons dark soya sauce
2 pieces star anise
1-inch-piece cinnamon bark
salt and sugar to taste
$\frac{3}{8}$ cup oil
3 cups water
3 shelled hard-boiled hen's eggs *or* 6 quail's eggs
chopped fresh chilli for garnish

Heat oil in a pan until it is very hot. Add the garlic and ginger and brown. Add the beef and stir until the meat changes colour. Add the star anise, cinnamon, sugar, salt, pepper and both kinds of soya sauce and water. Cover and gently simmer for 1 hour. Add the hard-boiled eggs whole and cook for another 20 minutes, by which time the eggs should have turned brown in the gravy. Serve garnished with chilli.

BRAISED STEAK CHINESE STYLE

2 lbs. beef fillet or fillet steak
1$\frac{1}{2}$ teaspoons salt
2 teaspoons sugar
1 tablespoon light soya sauce

4 tablespoons cornstarch
1 cup water
12 tablespoons water
4 tablespoons peanut oil
1 egg, beaten
4 tablespoons Worcestershire sauce

Trim the meat of all fat. Slice it into about 15 pieces. Mix all the
other ingredients together in a bowl and marinate the meat in
this mixture overnight. Next day remove the fillets, seal them well
by cooking for a few moments in a hot griddle or electric frying
pan. Add the sauce described below, cover the pan and allow
the fillets to braise until cooked. If you have used fillet steak,
this will be only a matter of minutes. You could, however, use
cheaper cuts of steak, like round steak or top round. These will
have to braise much longer before they are tender and you may
need to add a little more water to prevent the sauce getting too
thick.

Sauce

1 cup stock or water
$\frac{3}{4}$ teaspoon salt
5 teaspoons sugar
4 tablespoons Worcestershire sauce
$\frac{3}{4}$ teaspoon monosodium glutamate
4 teaspoons tomato sauce
1$\frac{1}{2}$ teaspoons sesame oil

Mix these ingredients together thoroughly and add to the pan
when the meat has been sealed.

CHOP SUEY (Serves 4 or 10)

Chop Suey is a dish which appears on the menu in almost every
Chinese restaurant in Western countries. It is no more truly
Chinese than the 'Chinoiserie' of 18th-century Europe. According to a friend of mine who is a Far Eastern historian, Chop Suey
was invented as a joke by a Chinese statesman visiting England in

1896. According to American food lore, it was invented in the late 1800's by a San Francisco Chinese cook who was ordered to serve food to a couple of ruffians who came into the restaurant at the end of the day. The cook had only a little bit of various dishes left, so he threw them together and Chop Suey was born. The name literally means 'rubbish' or 'food scraps.' This recipe, however, may be closer to home than most as it comes from a Chinese cooking teacher in Singapore.

1 yellow onion
1 small can button mushrooms
2 oz. Chinese dried mushrooms
⅜ lb. Chinese cabbage
3 oz. bamboo shoots
3 oz. green beans
6 fresh red chillies
¼ lb. pig's liver (optional)
¼ lb. (4 oz.) canned abalone, chicken or fish (only to be used if liver is not included)
¼ lb. pork, and a marinade made from:
   1½ teaspoons sherry
   1½ teaspoons light soya sauce
   1½ teaspoons cornstarch
1 lb. shrimp and a marinade for this of:
   1½ teaspoons peanut oil
   a little ginger juice
   ¾ teaspoon monosodium glutamate
¾ cup water
peanut oil or lard
2 cloves garlic, smashed and chopped

For the seasoning

2 teaspoons monosodium glutamate
4 teaspoons cornstarch
2 teaspoons salt
2 tablespoons water
2 tablespoons peanut oil
1½ teaspoons sugar
1 tablespoon light soya sauce
1 tablespoon Chinese oyster sauce

Cut the pork into shreds and steep in its marinade. Slice the liver, abalone, or fish into thin transverse slices, or cut the chicken into thin shreds. Soak the Chinese mushrooms until they are soft, remove their stalks, and halve them if they are large. Slice the vegetables and button mushrooms. Peel and devein the raw shrimp (use cooked only if necessary) and season with their marinade of oil and ginger juice and monosodium glutamate. Heat 1 tablespoon peanut oil or lard in a wok or frying pan. Stir-fry the shrimp. Lift them out and set aside.

Add more oil if necessary. Stir-fry the vegetables one kind at a time, lifting them out and setting them aside after each one is cooked. Fry the meats separately in the same way.

Heat another tablespoon of oil and fry the garlic until brown. Then put in all the fried ingredients. Add the seasoning, stir well until the mixture is slightly thickened and well mixed. Serve with plain boiled rice or noodles.

WILHELMINA'S PICKLED CHICKEN

This recipe was given to me by Mrs. Wilhelmina Sim of Kuching. It is a dish that has been cooked in her family for many years, and this is the first time the secret has been passed on.

2 lbs. chicken, cut into 3-inch pieces, including bones
5 tablespoons roasted coriander seeds
1 tablespoon cloves
4 cardamom pods
1½ teaspoons cumin seeds
1½ teaspoons turmeric
2-inch-piece cinnamon bark
12 dried hot chillies
1½ teaspoons ground nutmeg
2 medium yellow onions, finely chopped and the excess moisture
   squeezed out
4 cloves garlic, smashed and chopped
1-inch-piece green ginger, smashed and chopped
1 stalk lemon grass, finely sliced

5 tablespoons sugar
5 tablespoons white vinegar
salt to taste
5 tablespoons vegetable oil

Grind the coriander, cloves, cardamom, cumin, turmeric, cinnamon, chillies and nutmeg to a powder in an electric blender. Coat the pieces of chicken well with these ground spices and leave aside for at least 15 minutes.

Heat the oil in the pan and fry the onions, garlic, ginger and lemon grass until brown. Add the seasoned chicken and stir slowly for a while. Add 1 cup water and simmer until the chicken is tender. Then put in the vinegar, sugar and salt to taste. Stir and allow to cook fairly dry.

You can use meat instead of chicken for this dish.

FRIED EGGPLANT PATTIES

1 lb. eggplant, peeled and diced
1 egg, beaten
1½ teaspoons monosodium glutamate (optional)
2 tablespoons all-purpose flour
salt and pepper to taste
peanut oil

Boil the eggplant until tender. Drain and mash it. Allow to cool. Mix together the eggplant, egg, monosodium glutamate, salt, pepper and flour. Form into patties and fry in hot oil until brown.

Thailand

'PURE' Thai food is remarkably similar to the cuisine of the Javanese. It uses fiery chillies, sugar, garlic, blachan, lemon grass, and that recurring cousin of root ginger – laos, lengkuas or kah. Its nam priks are very like some of the sambals of Java and Bali, and it places a similar emphasis on the decorative presentation of vegetable dishes.

The Thais if anything go even further in decoration. Fruit and vegetable carving is traditionally a highly cultivated art. Anyone who has watched the infinite calm of a Thai woman carving a piece of young ginger root into the likeness of a crab with its pincers at the ready will bear witness to this. The possibilities of the art are infinite: pieces of cucumber skin are sculpted into leaf shapes and dropped into soups, fruits like melons and pineapples become magnificent boats or heads to decorate a festive table, vegetables are transformed into flowers. But perhaps most skilled of all is the art of building great floral pieces to be used as offerings in temples. There are various ritual models, sizes and patterns – from covered holy-water pots to dragon-topped pedestals made from lantana and amaranth blossoms, or bowls for holding flowers fashioned out of banana leaves. When placed on a stand along with incense sticks and candles these become an offering which shows reverence to the Buddhist monks or respect for one's elders. They are also used as a means of asking forgiveness from someone you have wronged, or of introducing yourself to a notable person. Garlands for weddings and welcoming ceremonies are made from gardenias and jasmine.

If there is any truth in the belief that food habits tend to reflect history, geography and style of life, then it is not altogether surprising to find such close parallels between Java and Thailand. Both can be described as agricultural, 'interior' societies. Both preserve a firm foundation of animism in the religions which

219

they have adopted from outside, and these religions have been modified accordingly. Nativistic ritual and festival play a large part in their lives, and there is little in the culture of either which can be called strictly secular.

Thai culture represents an amalgam of Indian and Chinese patterns, an amalgam which nevertheless merely underlies the distinctively Thai synthesis which is apparent today. The two influences are clearly reflected in Thai food. A typical main meal in a moderately well-off household will consist of rice and at least five other dishes. One of these will always be a curry, only a little modified from its original Indian form, and one or two will be of obvious Chinese origin: a kaeng chud soup, a stir-fried vegetable or a noodle dish. With these will appear the more 'native' tom yam or nam prik, or a meat flavoured with coriander root.

The characteristic and distinctive flavour of Thai food comes from three ingredients. These are fish sauce, which provides the saltiness desired in Thai cooking, coriander leaf, which is sprinkled over *everything*, and coriander root which is combined with garlic and black pepper to flavour meats before cooking. Fish sauce is apparently commonly used in Vietnam, but not in the southern lands of the region. Coriander leaf occurs in some Malay dishes but is by no means so universal a flavouring as it is to the Thais. This addiction often puzzles foreigners, for many of whom coriander leaf has a decidedly unpleasant taste: and though I have specified its use often in the recipes which follow, many of them will not suffer too much if it is left out or replaced by our more self-effacing parsley. However, they will not taste properly Thai. The coriander-root/garlic combination, on the other hand, is basic to most of the dishes in which it appears. To make anything of these, the reader must be prepared to cultivate her own coriander plants from seed.

Finally, although some old-time Thais still eat with their hands, as do their generation of Indonesians and Malays, it is nowadays very much the habit to use a spoon and fork where they are available. Since it is no simple matter to achieve neatness without starving if you use your hands, I should advise the setting of spoons and forks as the regular practice on a South-East Asian table.

A Thai meal develops, as I have pointed out, from the basic pattern of a bowl of cooked white rice, a *Kaeng phet* (curry), a soup, a vegetable dish with sauce (Nam Prik), and a selection from other kinds of dishes referred to by Thai cooks as 'side dishes.' These, however, are not the condiments and flavourings for curries we have come to recognize in Indian food but something rather more substantial. A minimum of five dishes plus rice is usually served at a proper Thai meal.

Here are a few suggested Thai menus:

1. White Rice
   Kaeng Phet Kai
   Kaeng Chud Pla
   Nam Prik Pak
   Pad Thua Ngork
   Tord Mun Kung

2. White Rice
   Kaeng Masaman
   Tom Yam Kung
   Nam Prik Deng Thai
   Yam Taeng
   Nua Tang *or* Luk Nua

3. White Rice
   Mi Krob
   Pla Tom Yam
   Kaeng Phet Nua
   Fan Taeng
   Yam Chomphu

4. White Rice
   Yam Yai
   Jang
   Kai Tom Kah *or* Kaeng
     Chud Kai Kabhed
   Kaeng Phet Nua
   Nam Prik Pak

5. White Rice
   Pad Wun Sen
   Kai Luk Koei
   Nam Prik Pao with Vegetables
   Kai Tord
   Kaeng Masaman.

Soups

There are two main types of soup eaten regularly in Thailand: Tom Yam and Kaeng Chud. The former is the more native, consisting of one kind of meat only, spiced in a characteristic fashion and cooked into a broth. Kaeng Chud is very different from this, being derived from the Chinese form. It is made without many spices and is mostly composed of one or two meats and some vegetable. The Thai addition to Kaeng Chud is coriander root. Mixed with the original garlic, this creates a unique taste and smell, and makes unnecessary the usual Chinese accompaniments of soya sauce or salted vegetables (tang chai). Thai soups should be served with rice and other dishes, as elsewhere in South East Asia.

If you have one, serve Tom Yams in a Chinese Steamboat. This is a brass pot with a vent through the middle with a grate in which hot charcoal is placed. The liquid cooks and is kept hot in a sort of moat around the vent.

TOM YAM KUNG (Shrimp, Crayfish or Lobster Tom Yam)

1½ lbs. raw shrimp, shelled and deveined
1 or 2 stalks lemon grass
2 teaspoons laos powder *or* 3 slices fresh laos
3–5 fresh chillies (preferably 'birdseye' chillies), according to taste
4 cups water
about 1½ tablespoons fish sauce, according to taste
1 tablespoon nam prik pao (see p. 242) *or* 1 tablespoon lemon or
    lime juice
3 lime leaves or citrus leaves

Cut the lemon grass into about 1½-inch pieces and smash the pieces with the side of a heavy knife or cleaver to let the aroma come out. Bring the water, lemon grass and laos to the boil and simmer gently for a while to allow the flavour of the spices to infuse. Add the fish sauce, then the shrimp and the chillies, which have been bruised but not chopped (unless they are long ones, in which case they can have been sliced in rounds). When the shrimp have turned pink, remove the saucepan from the stove, and stir in the Nam Prik Pao or lemon juice. Pour the soup into a tureen, and scatter the torn citrus leaves over the top. Serve some lemon or lime juice separately in a small jug for guests to help themselves. This is the 'pure' version of Tom Yam Kung.

When the Nam Prik Pao has been added to this Tom Yam it is sometimes turned into a sort of Thai minestra with the addition of fresh mushrooms, quartered tomatoes and chopped Chinese cabbage or chopped green onions. Garnish with chopped coriander leaves and fried garlic.

PLA TOM YAM (Fish Tom Yam)

1 lb. fish steaks or fillets (cod, sea bass or any sea fish)
2 teaspoons laos powder *or* 3 slices fresh laos
4 citrus or lime leaves, torn into pieces
1 stalk lemon grass, cut into 1-inch lengths, then smashed and
    bruised
4 cups water
½ cup lemon juice
1½ teaspoons ground chilli (optional)
3 or 4 teaspoons Nam Prik Pao (see p. 242)
fish sauce to taste (1–2 tablespoons)

For garnish

2 fresh red chillies, sliced into rounds
4 teaspoons chopped green onion
1 tablespoon chopped coriander leaf or parsley

Bring the water to the boil with the laos, lemon grass and citrus leaves. Drop in the fish pieces and simmer gently until cooked. Add the ground chilli, fish sauce and lemon juice. Remove the pot from the fire and stir in the nam prik pao. Pour into a tureen. Garnish with green onion, coriander leaf and sliced fresh chillies.

As a variation try this Tom Yam using whole cleaned baby squid.

KAI TOM KAH (Chicken Boiled with Laos)

1 small chicken ($1\frac{1}{2}$–2 lbs.), cut into curry pieces (see p. 24)
2 cups thin coconut milk
$\frac{1}{2}$ cup thick coconut milk
3 stalks lemon grass, cut into $1\frac{1}{2}$-inch lengths and bruised
1–$1\frac{1}{2}$ inches fresh laos, cut into thin slices, *or* 4 teaspoons laos powder
5 citrus or lime leaves

For garnish

a few fresh 'birdseye' chillies, bruised but not chopped, *or* 3 or 4 larger chillies, sliced into rounds
lemon or lime juice
fish sauce (optional)
coriander leaf (optional)

Put the chicken pieces into a wok or a saucepan, add the thin coconut milk, laos and lemon grass and bring to the boil. Simmer gently until the chicken is tender (about 30–45 minutes). Add the thick coconut milk, lime leaves, and salt or fish sauce to taste. Remove from the fire, pour into a soup tureen and garnish with chillies. Serve separate jugs of lemon or lime juice and fish sauce, and have some chopped coriander leaves or parsley available on another plate. Guests take some soup and add their own citrus juice, fish sauce and coriander leaves to taste.

KAENG CHUD PLA (Fish Ball Soup)

$1\frac{1}{2}$ cups raw flaked fish without skin or bones
$\frac{1}{2}$ lb. bean curd, cut into cubes (optional)
$\frac{1}{4}$ lb. pork chop meat, sliced

4 cloves garlic
½–1 tablespoon coriander root
a few peppercorns, ground
5 or 6 Chinese dried mushrooms
4 green onions with green leaves, chopped
1 tablespoon fish sauce
3 cups thin stock made with the fish bones, or plain water
chopped coriander leaves for garnish

Pound the garlic, coriander root and pepper together. Add the flaked fish and continue pounding until they are all mixed into a smooth paste. Form this into balls about the size of a shilling.

Soak the Chinese mushrooms until soft. Remove the hard stems, and quarter the mushrooms if they are large ones. Put the stock or water into a saucepan and bring it to the boil. Add the pork, bean curd, mushrooms and fish balls, and allow to simmer gently, covered, until the pork slices are cooked and the fish balls float on top. Add fish sauce and chopped green onions and stir. Remove from the fire, pour soup into a tureen, garnish with coriander leaves and serve hot.

KAENG CHUD KAI KABHED
(Chicken and Mushroom Soup)

1 medium chicken
1½ teaspoons salt
1 tablespoon fish sauce *or* light soya sauce
5 Chinese dried mushrooms
2 green onions (each cut diagonally into 3 pieces)
5 peppercorns, ground
3 cloves garlic
1 tablespoon coriander root
carved cucumber skin for garnish

Clean the chicken, removing the neck and feet, if necessary. (These may be added to the stock during cooking and removed before serving.) Put it into a saucepan with a lid, and cover with water. Add salt and green onions, cover and simmer for 2 hours or until the chicken is tender. Lift the chicken from the stock, remove the flesh from the bones and slice it. Keep aside. Strain the chicken stock and keep this aside too.

In the meantime, soak the Chinese mushrooms in warm water. Remove the hard stems and cut the mushrooms in half. Pound together the garlic, coriander root and pepper. Heat a little oil in a pan and fry them for a minute or two. Add the chicken meat and mix. Add the stock, fish sauce, and bring to the boil. Add the Chinese mushrooms, cover the pan and allow to simmer gently for a few minutes.

Pour into a tureen and garnish with pieces of green cucumber skin that have been carved into the shape of a leaf.

KAENG CHUD SAKU (Tapioca Soup) (Serves 4 or 8)

4–5 oz. uncooked ground pork *or* thinly sliced pork chop meat
4–5 oz. flaked crabmeat
3 oz. pearl tapioca
4½ cups chicken stock or bouillon
a dash of fish sauce to taste
3 or 4 stalks sweet Chinese cabbage, sliced, *or* chopped green onions
a dash of ground black pepper

Bring the stock to the boil. Pour a cupful over the ground pork through a strainer and back into the pot. This will prevent the pork from sticking together as it cooks. Now add the pork to the pot of stock on the stove. Season with fish sauce. Add the tapioca and simmer gently until the pork is cooked. Add the crabmeat and bring back to the boil. Add the Chinese cabbage, cover and simmer a minute until the vegetable is cooked but not soft. If you are using green onions instead, wait until you have poured the soup into a bowl and then scatter them over the top.

Serve this soup with small side dishes of fish sauce, thinly sliced garlic previously fried golden brown and crisp in peanut oil and drained, rounds of fresh red chilli in white vinegar and chopped coriander leaves. Guests garnish their individual bowls of soup with any of these according to their own taste.

MOH THONG LEUNG (The Brass Pot)
(Serves 5 or 10)

This dish, a thick broth with very little liquid, is named after the pot in which it is cooked and carried around the streets by hawkers. They announce their passage by striking a hollow bamboo instrument. Each one is identified by his special note. Moh Thong Leung is extremely popular with children, possibly because of its blandness.

1 lb. tripe
1½ lbs. leg or shin of beef
12-oz. can bamboo shoots
1 large beef bouillon cube
4½ teaspoons cornstarch
coriander leaves

Remove the gristle from the tripe and slice it finely. Cut any fat off the beef and slice it. Barely cover the tripe and the beef with water and boil gently for 2 hours. Allow the contents of the pot to cool and skim off the fat.

In the meantime drain the bamboo shoots and slice them into matchstick shapes. Put these in the pot and simmer the meat and bamboo shoots for another hour, adding the bouillon cubes near the end. Thicken the dish with cornstarch mixed with a little water. Remove from the fire and pour into a tureen.

Garnish this dish with chopped coriander leaves and serve with side dishes of fish sauce, fried garlic, and fresh chilli rounds in vinegar.

Fish

PLA PRIO WAN (Fried Fish with Sharp Sauce)

1 sea fish (for frying)
flour or cornstarch
1 clove garlic, smashed and chopped
3 green onions with green leaves, cut in 1-inch lengths
3 red fresh chillies, seeds removed, flesh cut and soaked into flower
   shapes
1 tablespoon smashed and chopped green ginger
1–4 tablespoons brown sugar, according to taste
1–4 tablespoons white vinegar, according to taste
5 tablespoons water
1½–3 teaspoons cornstarch for thickening
a dash of fish sauce or light soya sauce, according to taste
oil for deep frying

Clean and scale the fish. Make three or four slashes across each
side through to the bone. Rub with flour or cornstarch. Heat oil
in a wok or a pan and deep-fry the fish until brown and crisp.
Drain and keep warm. Pour all but a tablespoon of oil out of
the pan and return it to the stove. Fry the garlic until golden.
Add sugar, fish sauce and vinegar to taste. Then add water and
stir to mix. Put in the ginger, green onions and chillies. Finally
stir in the cornstarch and allow to thicken. Pour this sauce over
the whole fish and serve with plain rice.

TORD MUN KUNG (Fried Shrimp Balls)

1 lb. peeled and deveined raw shrimp
4 cloves garlic
¾ teaspoon peppercorns, ground
1 tablespoon coriander root (optional)
salt to taste
peanut oil for deep frying

Mince the shrimp with two Chinese cleavers or chop as finely as possible. In a mortar pound the garlic, coriander root, pepper and salt. Add the minced shrimp, pound and mix into a fine paste. Shape into small balls, which may be rolled in breadcrumbs if you prefer. Heat plenty of peanut oil in a wok or a pan and when it is very hot deep-fry the shrimp balls until they are brown. Drain and serve.

These can be partly cooked beforehand and deep-fried again at the last minute.

Poultry

KAENG PHET KAI (Chicken Curry)

1 medium chicken
1 cup thick coconut milk
2 cups thin coconut milk
a good handful of basil leaves, torn
a few whole fresh 'birdseye' chillies (optional)
a few lime or citrus leaves, torn
a few hard green baby eggplants (optional – this is only feasible if
 you grow eggplant)
fish sauce to taste

For the curry paste

$\frac{1}{2}$ stalk lemon grass, finely sliced (about 1 tablespoon)
1 slice laos *or* $\frac{1}{2}$ teaspoon laos powder
1 piece lime skin about 1-inch by $\frac{1}{2}$-inch, chopped or grated
5 or 6 small coriander roots, chopped
7 dried chillies
1 tablespoon peppercorns
2 tablespoons coriander seeds
2 teaspoons cumin seeds
1 tablespoon salt
$1\frac{1}{2}$ teaspoons blachan (shrimp paste)
8 cloves garlic
1 yellow onion, chopped

Grind the dry spices for the curry paste to a powder in an electric
blender. Add the coriander roots, garlic, onions, lime skin and
lastly blachan, and continue grinding to a fine paste. Add some
of the thick coconut milk if necessary to keep the blades turning.
Remove the paste from the blender to a bowl and mix in the
sliced lemon grass.

 Cut the chicken meat off the bones and then slice it. Bring the
thin coconut milk to the boil in a wok or a pan and drop in the

chicken meat. Allow to simmer gently, stirring frequently, until cooked (about 15–20 minutes). Remove from the fire.

Now lift out about one cup of the coconut milk and put it into another wok or shallow pan over a high heat and mix in the curry paste. Stir and cook until the coconut milk has evaporated and the spices are frying in the remaining oil. Continue stirring and frying until they smell cooked, then pour in little by little the rest of the thin coconut milk gravy from the chicken, stirring all the time. Cook until the gravy is thick and the oil 'comes out,' then add the chicken meat, the lime leaves, fresh chillies, eggplant and a spoonful of fish sauce. Leave to boil for a few minutes, then add the thick coconut milk and stir. Bring back to the boil and allow to thicken. Remove the pan from the stove, stir in the basil leaves, and serve.

KAO TOM KAI (Soft Boiled Rice with Chicken)

This dish is very suitable for invalids on a diet.

½ chicken
2 lbs. white rice
3–4 cups chicken stock
3 tablespoons finely chopped green onions
3 tablespoons sliced garlic
1 large lettuce, shredded
fish sauce or light soya sauce to taste
monosodium glutamate
peanut oil

Wash the rice thoroughly. Put it in a saucepan and add water to reach about 1½ inches above the rice. Boil until the rice is soft but not mushy. Remove from the fire and keep aside.

Remove the chicken meat from the bones. Finely chop it using two Chinese Cleavers and form into small balls. Bring the stock to the boil. Drop in the chicken balls, the rice, and fish sauce to taste, and boil until the chicken is cooked.

In the meantime, heat about 5 tablespoons peanut oil in a

wok and fry the garlic slices until they are light brown. Drain them and keep aside.

Line a tureen with shredded lettuce. Pour in the chicken and rice mixture with the stock. Sprinkle on the chopped green onions, fried garlic, a pinch of monosodium glutamate and some freshly ground pepper and serve.

KAI TORD (Fried Chicken)

2 chicken breasts
2 cloves garlic
¾ teaspoon freshly ground peppercorns
1 small coriander root
oil for deep frying

Grind the garlic, pepper and coriander root to a paste. Coat the chicken with this and leave to stand for at least 30 minutes.

Heat the oil in a wok or pan and when it is hot drop in the coated chicken pieces. Fry until the chicken is brown and tender, lowering the heat if necessary to prevent it burning. Drain the chicken pieces on paper toweling and serve with rice.

Meat

NUA TANG (Sweet Mince)

$\frac{3}{8}$ lb. frozen shrimp
$\frac{1}{2}$ lb. pork
1 cup thin coconut milk
$1\frac{1}{2}$ teaspoons salt
$1\frac{1}{2}$ teaspoons sugar (or according to taste)
1 red chilli, finely sliced
coriander leaves for garnish
ground black pepper

Put the coconut milk in a saucepan and allow to simmer. Mince or finely chop the pork and shrimp and drop them into the simmering coconut milk. When the meat is cooked season with salt, pepper and sugar, and add the chilli. Pour into a serving dish and decorate with coriander leaves.

This makes a delicious light luncheon dish served with Kao Thung (see p. 250).

LUK NUA (Thai Hamburgers or Meatballs)
(Serves 4 or 10)

1 lb. ground pork
1 lb. ground beef
6 cloves garlic, smashed and chopped
4 coriander roots, chopped
$1\frac{1}{2}$ teaspoons nutmeg
10 peppercorns, ground
4 tablespoons finely chopped onion
2 eggs, beaten
salt or fish sauce to taste
$1\frac{1}{2}$–3 teaspoons chopped coriander leaves

Pound the garlic, coriander roots and peppercorns to a paste. Combine all the ingredients, mix well and form into small

233

meatballs or large hamburgers. If they are small meatballs, they should be thinly coated with flour and deep fried in plenty of hot oil until brown, then drained. If they are to be served as regular-sized hamburgers they should be formed into patties and cooked on both sides on a lightly greased griddle or frying pan.

JANG (Seasoned Broil or Roast)

1 lb. pork chops or fillet steak
1 tablespoon coriander roots, chopped
$\frac{3}{4}$ teaspoon peppercorns, ground
4 cloves garlic
1 tablespoon fish sauce
5 teaspoons light soya sauce

Pound together the coriander roots, pepper and garlic to form a paste. Mix with the fish sauce and soya sauce. Spoon over the chops or steak and leave to marinate for at least 30 minutes. Lift out the meat and grill it over a charcoal fire or in the ordinary way.

A whole piece of pork loin or beef fillet can be seasoned in the same way and then roasted in the oven.

KAENG PHET NUA (Beef Curry)

Proceed as for chicken curry only using 1½ lbs. beef, diced. Add 6 cardamom pods and $\frac{3}{8}$ teaspoon mace to the curry paste, and cook in the same way as before. This method is also suitable for duck.

KAENG MASAMAN (Mussulman Curry)

2 lbs. beef, cut into cubes
somewhat over 4 cups thick coconut milk
1 cup roasted peanuts (optional)

tamarind water made from a piece of tamarind pulp the size of a
  walnut (see p. 37)
lemon or lime juice
sugar to taste

For the curry paste

7 dried chillies
¾ teaspoon whole black pepper
2 tablespoons coriander seeds
1 tablespoon cumin seeds
2 tablespoons chopped green ginger
1 tablespoon finely sliced lemon grass
1½ teaspoons salt
5 cloves
1-inch-stick cinnamon bark
2 yellow onions, finely chopped
5 cloves garlic, smashed and chopped
5 cardamom pods
¾ teaspoon nutmeg
a pinch of mace
¾ teaspoon blachan or shrimp paste

Smear the pan with oil and roast all the dry ingredients for the
curry paste together until they smell cooked. Remove and grind
to a powder in a blender. Heat a little oil in a pan and fry the
onions, garlic, ginger and blachan until they are soft. Add these to
the blender and continue grinding to a smooth paste. Mix this
with the sliced lemon grass.

  Bring the coconut milk to the boil and add the beef and peanuts.
Simmer until the beef is tender. (This will depend on the cut of
the beef, but for shoulder or round steak, say, 45 minutes.)
Remove the meat and continue boiling the gravy until it is reduced by one third. Stir the curry paste into this. Return the
meat and simmer until the sauce is smooth and thick. Finally
stir in the tamarind water, lime juice and sugar to taste, and
serve.

LAHP ISAN (Eastern Spiced Meat)

Lahp is one of the favourite dishes of North Thailand. The classic version is nearly always mentioned in tourist articles and visitors' descriptions of this area, but, because of its rather uncompromising quality for the foreign palate, actual recipes for the Northern Lahp are hard to come by. It consists of quite raw beef, pounded to a hash and mixed with fresh blood and rendered explosive by the addition of enormous quantities of the hottest chilli.

This recipe is a tamer version of the dish used in the Eastern part of the country.

1 lb. ground round steak
3 stalks lemon grass, finely sliced
2 yellow onions, chopped fine
1 heaping tablespoon of rice
6 dried small 'birdseye' chillies
6 fresh green chillies, sliced
1½ sweet green bell peppers, chopped, with the seeds removed
30 mint leaves
juice of 1½ lemons
fish sauce or salt to taste

Roast the rice in a dry pan on top of the stove until it is opaque and a very pale yellow in colour, then transfer it to a mortar and pound it roughly until it is the consistency of coarse sand. Roast the dry chillies in the same pan, and grind them.

Boil about 2½ cups water, throw in the meat, and stir it lightly just until the meat changes colour, then drain well, and put away the stock for some other purpose. Transfer the meat to a serving dish, pour the lemon juice over it, mix in half the mint leaves and all the other ingredients. Season to taste with fish sauce or plain salt, decorate the platter with the remaining mint leaves, and serve with plain boiled rice and a Thai salad.

Vegetables

Thai vegetable dishes seem to fall into three main categories. They are *yams* (literally, to mix with the hands), which are a sort of local tossed salad, raw or boiled vegetables served with a fiery chilli-based sauce (Nam Prik), or more Chinese-inspired steamed vegetables, usually stuffed. I shall deal with these under their general headings.

YAMS

I. YAM YAI (Big Salad) (Serves 4 or 10 people)

1 lb. cooked shrimp
2 loin pork chops
1 chicken breast (optional)
3 small unpeeled cucumbers, sliced
1 small fresh onion *or* 1 pickled onion, finely chopped
10 small round radishes
3 oz. bean sprouts, blanched
1 oz. Chinese vermicelli
1 tablespoon Chinese cloud ear or tree fungus
6 sprigs mint
freshly ground black pepper

For the dressing

1 fresh red chilli, finely chopped
4½ teaspoons fish sauce
¾ teaspoon white sugar
1 small clove garlic
juice of 1 small lemon

For garnish

3 hard-boiled eggs
2 or more fresh chillies
torn coriander leaves or parsley

Peel and chop the shrimp, unless they are small ones, which can be left whole. Drop the pork chops into boiling water, and simmer until well done. Allow to cool in the water. Remove them, cut off the skin and bone, and slice the remaining meat into fine strips. Steam the chicken breast, allow to cool, and cut the meat into shreds.

Top and tail the radishes, and carve them into flowerets. Pull the tops off the bean sprouts. Soak the vermicelli in cold water until it is soft, drain and cut up. Similarly soak the cloud ear fungus, and drain. Put all these ingredients with the onion and the cucumber into a serving bowl, add the mint sprigs, season with freshly ground black pepper, and toss well in a dressing made from the lemon juice, the garlic crushed with salt, sugar, finely chopped fresh chilli and the fish sauce.

Decorate the salad with quarters of boiled egg, fresh chillies that have been cut with a needle and soaked into flowers (see p. 23), and torn coriander leaves or parsley.

II. YAM CHOMPHU (Salad of Tart Fruit)

2 large tart apples (McIntosh), green mangoes *or* 1 small pineapple, peeled and finely sliced
$\frac{1}{8}$ lb. pork chop meat, boiled for 15 minutes, cooled, and thinly sliced
$\frac{1}{8}$ lb. cooked shrimp, peeled and deveined
juice of $\frac{1}{2}$ lemon *or* equivalent tamarind water
$1\frac{1}{2}$ teaspoons sugar
3 or more teaspoons fish sauce, according to taste

Make a dressing from the lemon juice, sugar, and fish sauce. Pour over the other ingredients in a large bowl and toss well.

III. YAM TAENG (Crisp Salad)

about 8 oz. crisp vegetables, cut into strips or slices (cucumber, water chestnuts, radishes, lettuce, individually or mixed)

2 tablespoons sliced cooked shrimp, pork or crab meat *or*
   2 tablespoons ground dried shrimp
½ yellow onion, finely chopped
juice of ½ lemon
1½ teaspoons sugar
1 tablespoon fish sauce
salt to taste
a pinch of ground chilli (optional)

For garnish

sprigs of mint or coriander leaves
1 tablespoon fried garlic slices
fresh chillies cut and soaked into flower shapes

Place the vegetables, meat and onion in a salad bowl. Mix the lemon juice, sugar, salt, fish sauce and ground chilli into a dressing and toss with the salad ingredients. Garnish with fried garlic, mint or coriander sprigs and chilli flowers.

SOM TOM (Another salad)

½ lb. finely shredded vegetables (a mixture of cucumber, celery, green pawpaw, raw beans and a little raw cabbage)
2 firm tomatoes, quartered
lettuce leaves

Dressing

Make a dressing *according to taste* from lots of freshly ground black pepper, garlic, ground chilli, brown sugar, fish sauce and lemon juice. The dressing should be quite sweet and hot, so start your experiment with proportions something like this:

2 teaspoons fish sauce
1 tablespoon pepper
1½ teaspoons ground chilli
4½ teaspoons sugar
3 cloves garlic
juice of 1 lemon

Go on adjusting to taste from there.

Toss the shredded vegetables and tomatoes in this and serve on a bed of lettuce leaves.

NAM PRIK

Probably the most universal Thai dish of all would be one of the varieties of Nam Prik or hot sauce accompanied by vegetables either raw, boiled, or fried in batter, singly or in a tastefully arranged collection. All Thais eat these more often than anything else for ordinary family meals, and different versions of the basic sauce appear in all parts of the country.

As well as with vegetables, Nam Priks are commonly served with varieties of salted fish that have been roasted or steamed and fried. Pla tu, a favourite, is in fact small bonito that has been salted and smoked. After being bought in the market it is first steamed and then fried in oil. This accompanies the vegetables and the Nam Prik with plain rice. Boiled shrimp, any smoked fish or dry herring could be substituted.

This is the 'pure' way to serve Nam Prik, but Thais nowadays tend to be very free and easy with these sauces. They add them to cooked dishes as a sort of spices 'short cut' (see, for instance, the use of Nam Prik Pao in soups), and use them in thin versions as a sauce for rice or noodles. Where such perversions are possible I have said so at the end of the recipe.

I. NAM PRIK PAK (Raw Vegetables with Basic Hot Sauce)

The vegetables used in Thailand for this dish would be many and various. They would probably include all sorts of roots, leaves, tubers, and even flowers, and would cover just about the whole range of the taste and colour spectra. There would be something sweet, something sour, something salty, things of different textures, and many colours. All would be very fresh. And almost certainly they would include some of the green mango the Thais are so fond of. This is crisp and almost painfully tart. Unless you live in the tropics where mangoes flourish, it is difficult to find a substitute for this fruit. Either slices of really tart cooking apples or raw gooseberries are probably the nearest thing. At any rate, you can afford to experiment to your heart's content with vegetables for a Nam Prik.

As a start I suggest the following: watercress, red radishes, strips of bamboo shoot, cucumber with skin, slices of young eggplant (fried in butter until brown), celery strips, green beans, Chinese cabbage, carrot strips, the leaves and sliced root of fennel, mustard greens, preserved ginger, and so on. Arrange these in sections around a large serving platter and place a bowl of Nam Prik in the middle, garnished with a sprig or two of mint.

Sauce

6 dried shrimp, pounded in a blender
2 cloves garlic
1½ teaspoons blachan, roasted in foil (see p. 28)
dried chillies to taste
juice of 1 lime or ½ lemon
1 tablespoon sugar
1 tablespoon fish sauce

Grind chillies to a powder in an electric blender. Add all the other ingredients and blend to a thick sauce. All amounts may be changed according to taste.

II. NAM PRIK DENG THAI (Hot Sauce with Boiled Vegetables)

Any vegetable or group of vegetables may accompany this Nam Prik. They are lightly boiled in water or thin coconut milk first, drained, then served with plain rice and the sauce. If you use more than one vegetable, boil each variety separately and serve in separate mounds on the dish.

Sauce

5 dried red chillies (the long kind), soaked and softened in water for about 30 minutes, then drained
1 large yellow onion, chopped
3 cloves garlic
1 tablespoon blachan, roasted in foil (see p. 28)
salt

Mix all these ingredients together in a blender, adding a little water if you prefer a thinner consistency. If you intend to keep the Nam Prik for any length of time, do not add salt.

III. NAM PRIK PAO (Roasted Hot Sauce)

5 red dried chillies (the long ones)
3 large cloves garlic
2 medium yellow onions *or* 5 Bombay onions, if available, *or* 5 shallots
1 tablespoon blachan
tamarind water made from a piece tamarind pulp the size of a walnut
1 tablespoon brown sugar

This Nam Prik can only be made when you have a charcoal barbecue or a low wood fire burning. Put the whole unpeeled onions and garlic on a rack near the ashes over the fire and roast them until they are quite black on the outside and well cooked inside. Wrap the blachan in foil and roast it, then remove the foil. Roast the whole chillies in the same way as the onions. Put everything into an electric blender and grind to a thick paste.

This is the basic Nam Prik Pao. Sometimes a variation is produced which includes roasted peanuts and roasted dried shrimp, ground. Nam Prik Pao is eaten with plain rice and unspiced vegetables in the normal way. It is added to Tom Yams. An excellent fried rice can be made by simply frying cold cooked rice in a little oil, adding Nam Prik Pao to taste as it cooks, and also fish sauce. Stir everything well to mix as it cooks. Try Nam Prik Pao on rounds of toast as canapés or with white crusty bread and butter.

In Thailand Nam Prik Pao is usually bought already cooked and packed in jars. It is a good idea to make a large quantity (at least five times the quantities of this recipe) and store for future use. To do so, fry the paste in a little oil and store in a covered jar in the refrigerator.

IV. NAM PRIK DENG CHIENGMAI
(Northern Hot Sauce)

5 dried red chillies (the long ones)
1 very small yellow onion *or* 2 Bombay onions, if available, *or* 2
    shallots
6 cloves garlic
1 small pla ra (a local fermented fish) *or* any kind of salted fish
    (herring) *or* 2 teaspoons blachan roasted and blended with 1
    tablespoon fish sauce

Roast the chillies, onion, and garlic over a charcoal fire in the same way as for Nam Prik Pao but not so black. If you have pla ra or other small fish, remove the flesh from the bones, chop it, wrap in foil and roast over the coals. Remove foil wrapper. Combine everything in a blender and mix to a paste.

    This paste can be eaten with anything. In Chiengmai people are especially fond of it with glutinous rice which is used throughout the whole of Northern Thailand in place of the normal rice. It also serves as a spices base for many cooked dishes. One of these is Nam Prik Ong, the recipe which follows.

V. NAM PRIK ONG

1 tablespoon Nam Prik Deng Chiengmai (above)
¾ lb. lean pork, ground or chopped
4 or 5 ripe tomatoes, peeled
peanut oil

Heat a little oil in a wok or a saucepan and fry the Nam Prik a little. Add the pork and stir until it changes colour. Chop and

243

drain the tomatoes, then add them. Cover and cook until done, adding water only if the sauce is too dry.

This sauce can be served in numerous ways – as a dip with packaged fried pork rinds or potato chips, as a sauce over boiled noodles or spaghetti, on toast or canapés, or with plain rice.

FAN TAENG (Stuffed Zucchini)

1 young zucchini, about 9 inches long
½ lb. finely chopped pork
1–2 cloves garlic
a pinch of black pepper
a dash of fish sauce
meat from 1 cooked crab *or* 1 small can crab meat
a few shrimp, cooked and peeled
coriander leaf and fried garlic for garnish

Cut off the ends of the zucchini and carefully remove pith and seeds. Stuff the hollow cylinder with the pork, chopped garlic, pepper and fish sauce. Replace the ends of the zucchini and steam it until cooked in a little water or stock. Serve sliced in rounds and strewn with crab meat and shrimp in an attractive dish. Garnish with coriander leaf and fried garlic.

PAD THUA NGORK (Fried Bean Sprouts)

⅛ lb. raw pork cut from the loin, finely sliced
4 cloves garlic, smashed and chopped
¼ lb. raw shrimp, peeled and deveined
½ lb. fresh bean sprouts
fish sauce to taste
sugar to taste
a dash of ground black pepper
1 tablespoon lard

Clean and wash the bean sprouts. Heat the lard in a wok or pan and fry the garlic until it is golden brown. Add the pork and stir-fry until cooked. Add the shrimp and stir-fry. Add seasonings to taste, and then, when everything is very hot, add the bean sprouts. Stir-fry until the bean sprouts are cooked but still crisp.

Sundries

KAI LUK KOEI (Son-in-Law Eggs)

duck's or hen's eggs
oil for deep frying
brown sugar
fish sauce to taste
sliced fresh chilli and fried onion flakes (see p. 22) for garnish

Boil the eggs until they are hard but not like bullets (about 6–8 minutes). The yolk should not be fluid but it should be tender. Cool the boiled eggs in cold water, then peel and cut them in half. Heat sufficient oil or lard in a wok or saucepan to deep-fry the boiled eggs, flat side down, until the outside is golden. Lift, drain, and keep warm on a plate with the yolk side uppermost.

Leaving only a small amount of oil (about 1 tablespoon) in the pan, melt sufficient brown sugar in it to form a sauce to cover the eggs. If its consistency is too thick, add a little water. Then add fish sauce to taste, and stir as it bubbles for about 5 minutes or until you have a thick, brown, well-blended sauce. Pour over the eggs and garnish with slices of fresh red chilli and fried onion flakes.

MI KROB (Crisp Fried Noodles)

1 lb. Chinese rice vermicelli
2 oz. each of sliced pork chop meat, chopped raw shrimp, chicken, crab or squid, *or* any combination thereof
1 tablespoon chopped garlic
1 tablespoon chopped onion
5 teaspoons pickled garlic,* sliced (optional)

*To make pickled garlic, peel whole cloves of garlic and drop them into a simmering syrup mixture made from vinegar, sugar and salt to taste. Return to boiling point, cool, and store in sterilized screw-top jars until they are ready (at least one week).

4½ teaspoons grated grapefruit skin or orange skin
3 oz. fresh bean sprouts, washed
5 tablespoons lemon juice
1 tablespoon yellow soya bean paste (available canned in Chinese
    grocers) *or* 4 tablespoons finely sliced soya bean curd
vinegar and fish sauce to taste (a dash of each)
5 tablespoons sugar
4 eggs
fresh red chillies, sliced in rounds
coriander leaves, chopped
peanut oil for deep frying

Put plenty of oil for deep frying in a wok and make it very hot.
Take the vermicelli *straight from the package* (do not soak it),
break off a handful and put this into the oil, stirring as it cooks
crisp and golden brown. Lift out and allow to drain thoroughly
on paper, repeating the process until all the vermicelli is fried.
Keep aside.

In another wok or pan heat 4 tablespoons oil and fry the onions
and garlic until they are brown. Then put in the meats and stir-
fry until they are cooked. Add the soya bean paste, lemon juice,
sugar, a dash of vinegar and a dash of fish sauce and stir. Break
in the eggs and stir the mixture until it is set, then continue cooking for about 5 minutes until everything is dry and oil remains
separate.

Adjust the seasonings to make sure that the dish is correctly
salt, sour, and sweet (it should be all three), adding more sugar,
vinegar, or fish sauce if necessary. Finally stir in the fried vermicelli, mix well and lift the pan off the stove.

Dish the mixture out on a large serving plate and garnish with
pickled garlic, grapefruit skin, sliced chilli, and coriander leaf.
Arrange the cold bean sprouts decoratively at the edge of the plate
and serve immediately.

KAO PAD THAI (Thai Fried Rice)

5 cups cold cooked rice
2 cups chopped yellow onions

¼ lb. chopped green onions
1 lb. sliced raw pork, shrimp and crab meat in combination
4 tablespoons chopped coriander leaf
4 eggs
2 tablespoons fish sauce
4 tablespoons light Chinese soya sauce
tomato ketchup to taste
a little peanut oil

Heat the oil in a wok and fry the onions until they are soft but not brown. Add the meat and fish and stir-fry until cooked. Break in the eggs and stir everything together until set. Put in the rice and stir until it is well coated. Sprinkle over the fish sauce, soya sauce, and enough tomato sauce to make the dish red in colour. This is the distinguishing feature of Thai fried rice as opposed to Chinese. Continue stirring until everything is hot and well mixed, adding chopped green onion and coriander leaf just before serving.

PAD WUN SEN (Fried Vermicelli)

1 lb. Chinese vermicelli
½ lb. pork loin or pork chop meat, sliced
½ lb. raw shrimp, peeled, deveined and chopped
4 green onions, sliced into 1-inch lengths
1 clove garlic, chopped
½ cup cloud ear or tree fungus
1 carrot, cut into matchstick lengths
pepper, fish sauce, vinegar, sugar to taste
2 tablespoons peanut oil
coriander leaves for garnish

Soak the cloud ear or tree fungus in warm water until soft, then wash and drain. Also soak the vermicelli in warm water for 15 minutes and drain well. Heat the oil in a wok and fry the garlic until soft. Add the pork and stir-fry. When it is cooked, add the shrimp and stir-fry, then the carrots, green onions and seasonings. Add the vermicelli and mix well, stirring until everything is hot. Arrange on a serving plate and garnish with coriander leaves.

SAKU SAI MOOH (Stuffed Sago)

4 tablespoons peanut oil
1 lb. ground pork
½ cup finely chopped roasted peanuts
4 tablespoons finely chopped onions
1 tablespoon salt
1 teaspoon pepper
½ cup sugar
just under 1¼ cups boiling water
¾ cup sago *or* tapioca, if sago not available

Heat the peanut oil, sauté the onion for one minute, and add the pork, sugar, salt and pepper. Cook over a medium heat, stirring frequently for 10–15 minutes, then add the peanuts. Wash the sago and put into boiling water. Cook over a low heat stirring frequently for 2 minutes. Remove from the stove and leave until cool.

Take one spoonful of sago and spread out into a flat, round shape. Put some of the pork and peanut mixture into the middle and fold in half or cover with another round shape. Steam the sago cakes for about 15 minutes. Serve hot or cold with lettuce or other salad.

MAH HO (Galloping Horses)

1 can sliced pineapple or sliced fresh pineapple
4 tablespoons peanut oil
1 lb. ground pork
½ cup finely chopped roasted peanuts
4 tablespoons finely chopped onions
1 tablespoon salt
1 teaspoon pepper
¼ cup sugar
1 shredded red chilli, chopped mint leaves or coriander leaves for
  garnish

Heat the peanut oil, sauté the onion for one minute and add the pork, salt, sugar and pepper. Cook over a medium heat, stirring frequently, for 10–15 minutes and add the peanuts. Spoon a layer of the mixture on top of each pineapple slice. Garnish with chilli and mint leaves or chopped coriander leaves.

The pineapple slices can be cut into smaller cubes and the coated pieces then served as an hors d'oeuvre.

KAO THUNG (Rice Crisps)

This is a recipe for using up the layer of hard rice that is sometimes left adhering to the saucepan when rice is cooked by the evaporation method.

Remove the caked rice from the saucepan in chunks, and allow them to dry out completely. They will be ready in a week or two! Deep-fry the rice chunks in oil, and drain them on paper toweling. Kao Thung makes a delicious crisp accompaniment to Nua Tang.

MIANG KAI KRATHONG KRORP
(Thai Cocktail Cups)

For this recipe you need a special mould for making cocktail cups. This resembles a small ladle with a fluted cup at the base and a long handle that allows you to hold the base in boiling oil without burning your hands. I have seen moulds like this in quite ordinary hardware stores.

Batter for the cups

½ cup rice flour
½ cup wheat flour
about 3 cups medium-thin coconut milk
peanut oil for deep frying

Sift and mix the two kinds of flour in a bowl, adding the coconut milk gradually, being careful to stir out all lumps, until you have a thin batter.

Heat plenty of peanut oil in a wok or a saucepan for deep frying. Let the mould stand in the oil as it heats. Remove the mould when hot, empty it of all oil, then dip it into the batter allowing it to become coated with the mixture. Return the coated mould to the pan of hot oil and allow the batter to cook, easing the cup off the mould as it sets and allowing it to finish cooking in the oil as you repeat the process. Remove the cups when they are cooked and drain them thoroughly.

(N.B. If you use a hollow mould, you will end up with two cups per dip – one on the outside of the mould and one on the inside, unless you avoid immersing the hot iron in the batter completely. It would probably be simpler to stop short of the upper rim of the mould and concentrate on having only one cup at a time to handle.)

For the filling

5 teaspoons grated grapefruit or orange skin
8 oz. roasted peanuts
3 oz. pickled garlic (see p. 246)
5 tablespoons chopped yellow onions
5 tablespoons finely chopped green ginger
1 lb. steamed chicken meat, minced or ground
1 tablespoon sugar
1½ teaspoons salt
juice of 1 lemon *or* 2 limes
1 tablespoon white rice that has been dry-fried until brown, and
    then crushed to a sandy consistency (optional)
fresh chilli, sliced in rounds, and chopped coriander leaf or parsley,
    for garnish

In a bowl mix together the sugar, salt, lemon or lime juice, pounded rice and chicken. Take a cup in one hand, put in a little each of the peanuts, ginger, onion, pickled garlic and grapefruit skin. Cover with a spoon of chicken mixture and garnish the top with a slice of chilli and some chopped coriander leaf or parsley. Repeat the process until all the cups and filling are used up.

SOME SUGGESTIONS FOR SNACKS AND
COCKTAIL SAVOURIES

KAO POT PING

10 ears of corn, husks and silks removed
1 cup thin coconut milk
salt

Roast the corn over a charcoal fire, dipping it in the salted coconut
milk two or three times during the cooking.

KLUEY CHAP

For this recipe and the next you will need a pan of peanut oil on
the fire for deep frying. Slice skinned green bananas thinly and
deep-fry. Drain.

PAKAH

Soak a handful of brown dried lima beans in water overnight.
Drain and dry them, and deep-fry in peanut oil. Sprinkled with
salt, these make a pleasant accompaniment to drinks.

Index

255

257

259